Journey of Conscience

Young People Respond to the Holocaust

**Leatrice Rabinsky
Gertrude Mann**

COLLINS
Cleveland • New York

Published by William Collins Publishers, Inc.
Cleveland • New York

First published 1979

Copyright © 1979 by Leatrice Rabinsky and
Gertrude Mann

Library of Congress Cataloging in Publication Data
Rabinsky, Leatrice, 1927-
    A journey of conscience.
    1. Holocaust, Jewish (1939-1945)—Poland. 2. Poland
—Description and travel—1945-   3. Israel—Descrip-
tion and travel. 4. Rabinsky, Leatrice, 1927-   5. Mann,
Gertrude, 1929-   I. Mann, Gertrude, 1929-   joint
author. II. Title.
D810.J4R32   940.53'1503'924   79-17418
ISBN 0-529-05679-8

Printed in the United States of America

CONTENTS

		Foreword	5
1	•	A Different Journey	7
2	•	Lidice, a City Destroyed	15
3	•	No Names in Terezin	21
4	•	Twelve Hours to Warsaw	31
5	•	The Warsaw Ghetto	35
6	•	Bertha Lautman, Our Survivor	41
7	•	We Must Remember Auschwitz	51
8	•	The Holy Books of Cracow	61
9	•	On to Israel	65
10	•	Christmas in Bethlehem	71
11	•	Jerusalem, Yad Vashem	75
12	•	Jerusalem, a Free Day	83
13	•	A Warsaw Ghetto Hero	89
14	•	Kibbutzim	95
15	•	Amsterdam, Holland	101
16	•	Heading Home	111

Foreword

Eighteen voices speak from the pages of this book. They tell of a unique journey into the past and of their commitment to the future.

Bertha Lautman was the only one on the journey who actually lived through the Holocaust. The two teachers were fortunate to have been teenagers in America during this time. Several of the students had lost grandparents, aunts, uncles, and cousins in the ghettoes and concentration camps. Thus, each of us brought a different perspective to this journey whether it was a historical investigation, a search for ancestral roots, or a religious conviction. We joined as a family: praying with the remnants in Prague, staring in disbelief at the bleakness that once was Lidice, crying together at the Memorial in Auschwitz, rejoicing with Antek Zuckerman at the rebirth in Israel, and sharing our hope for tomorrow at the Anne Frank House in Amsterdam.

Our promise to convey what we have seen continues to be fulfilled. Students, survivors, and teachers have spoken in eleven cities in the United States and Canada before thousands of people of all faiths. Small rural communities who had never heard of the word "Holocaust" now know about tyranny and dehumanization and how world apathy can contribute to world catastrophe.

They have learned of Hitler's "final solution" for the Jewish people, the greatest planned genocide in man's history. They have learned that millions of Christians, those who opposed Nazi philosophy, those who did not conform to the Aryan myth, were also destroyed. Our students have discovered how education can be distorted. Who, after all, were those with the brilliant minds that devised efficient plans for massive deportation by train and designed the blueprints for concentration camp gas chambers and crematoria?

On college campuses, the students became emissaries organizing Holocaust seminars, helping to institute courses and planning programs for Days of Remembrance. Trinity College, Tufts, North-

5

western University, Youngstown, Boston, Ohio State, and Miami Universities have all had active programs because of the efforts of our students.

Journey members have published in newspapers, magazines, and college journals. A film-strip cassette media package created from slides taken by the students and entitled, *Journey of Conscience, A New Generation Responds to the Holocaust* has had national distribution. One student from Northwestern University has been instrumental in organizing a rebuttal to a professor on campus who has written a book denying that the Holocaust ever took place.

Three years after the first journey we are still moving forward. Journey of Conscience II became a reality in June 1979 when twenty students of different faiths embarked on another mission of remembrance and commitment.

We, the teachers, affirm our faith in the young people of today. Given an opportunity to explore and use their strengths, informed students will be the greatest force for good in this world.

What we have learned from the Holocaust is that we cannot stand idly by. The lesson that we and the students have learned is this: *We Shall Never Forget.*

Although we can never truly understand what happened, we can recognize some of mankind's mistakes by confronting the past. We pray that this will guide us in using our education for good so that our lives will be forces for justice, morality, and freedom.

May 1979   LEATRICE RABINSKY
                                            GERTRUDE MANN

1

A Different Journey

Craig Spiegel was always bright, meticulous, well-organized, and on time. Once in the ninth grade when our English class was studying *A Tale of Two Cities*, he proposed the most challenging and creative project, a huge made-to-scale model of La Guillotine, "the national cure for headaches," which he and Jon Kushner brought to class long before the other students had even thought of any ideas for their projects.

How exciting it was, then, three years later, to find Craig in the first "Literature of the Holocaust" class in Heights High. Craig had selected this course because his entire family on both his mother's and father's sides had been part of the Holocaust experience. Not only would Craig become one of the outstanding research students in the class, but he would often be the stalwart, reliable person when it came to class efforts such as the first Holocaust Community Forum, or the student poetry publication in memory of the children of the Holocaust.

Craig invited his mother to speak to our class about her teen-age war experiences. Thea Spiegel was one of the first persons in the community who was willing to open old wounds and to relive the dark years of the late thirties and early forties.

In looking back, it was perhaps during one of those meetings with Holocaust survivors that the idea for the "journey of conscience" began to take form. When the plans for the journey finally

7

materialized in the spring of 1975, it was natural that Craig was one of the students whom we consulted. He was well-organized and could make thoughtful plans.

Craig also knew about other journeys from his own parents. Craig's grandfather, Jakob Lange, had been a publisher in Danzig of *Der Folk Sturmer*, a Social-Democratic newspaper. A cultured, educated, socially-active family, the Langes were well aware of the dangers of Nazism in Europe, and Jakob and Erna Lange had tried to get visas to the United States for themselves and their daughters. In the summer of 1939, they received one visa only, which was given to Thea, the middle child. And so, at age twelve, Thea Lange's journey began, first by train to Rotterdam, then across the channel to England. Thea was placed in an English orphanage where she remained until the beginning of the German bombardment of London. At that time she went to live with a foster family in the English countryside, and soon after, with an older couple. At age fifteen Thea had to leave school and go to work to be self-supporting. During the Blitz of London in 1944, Thea's office building was bombed. She lost her sight in one eye when hit by flying glass which detached her retina. After the war, in November 1946, Thea took another journey, this time to the United States aboard the Queen Elizabeth.

Craig says, "My mother was one of the lucky ones during the war." His grandfather, Jakob Lange, was arrested in Danzig in September 1939, because he had published an anti-Nazi book describing the military invasion of Austria. Jakob died from hard labor in the Shtuthopf concentration camp. In October 1939, Thea's mother, Erna Lange, and her two sisters began their journey by illegal ship from Italy to Palestine. They were halted mid-voyage by a British ship and sent to Mauritius in the Indian Ocean. Sick with malaria, they remained there until after the war, finally arriving in Palestine in 1945. Grandmother Erna, both sisters, and their families now live in Moshav Moledet in northern Israel.

On December 17, 1975, a Wednesday evening, we were ready to begin our journey. In the KLM lounge, Craig's cousin, Helen Senders, came to wish us well as we sat waiting for our overseas flight. Much to our surprise KLM had mounted a sign reading,

"Journey of Conscience," above their ticket counter. Helen, a cousin of Craig's father's, Martin Spiegel, said that no such sign had announced their journey in the summer of 1944. She and her mother, Craig's grandmother and four other aunts and uncles with their spouses and children had all been taken on the Hungarian transports to the Auschwitz concentration camp. "We were taken in wagons, you know, the cattle cars, air-tight. We were suffocating, mad with hunger and thirst." Most adults with young children were taken directly to the gas chambers. Only the teen-aged children, and Helen was one of them, were sent to labor details and ultimately survived.

Craig's father, Martin Spiegel, had an unusual war odyssey. Born in a rural area of Czechoslovakia, he was able to leave Europe in 1940. The Germans had not yet invaded Hungary, Romania, and the surrounding area. Soon after he arrived in this country, Martin Spiegel joined the United States Army and was sent overseas to the North African theater of war. He also served in Italy. At the end of the war, Martin went back to his village and found a few surviving relatives. He brought them to Italy and made certain that they boarded the proper transports for Palestine. Martin returned to the United States, worked as an engineer and met Thea Lange. They were married in December 1947. They had one daughter and three sons. Martin Spiegel died of cancer when Craig was only six years old.

Craig grew up quickly. His serious manner and air of responsibility always seemed to pervade, even during moments of fun and excitement. As we boarded the posh 747 we were all emotional, anxious, noisy, and even frightened. It was Craig who helped get us settled and he even distributed the pre-Journey questionnaires which had been prepared for the students.

The first question was, "What are you thinking and feeling as we start this unique journey?"

Here are some answers. Lou wrote, "I feel as if I'm going not only for myself, but for my parents, family, friends, and many others who know little about the Holocaust . . . feelings of fright, mourning, shame. Shame, I can't describe what for, maybe that it all happened, maybe that it didn't happen to me." Ronnie, whose parents are also survivors, wrote, "My first thought is of my parents' homeland.

Both my parents and most of my relatives were in concentration camps. I want to see what they have always talked about." Amy reflected, "I don't think I'd be on this plane if I hadn't studied the Holocaust. It's not the kind of class you take and forget." Scott's answer was to the point, "To learn about the deeds of the era, we must see every place firsthand." Craig's attitude to the journey was his longstanding commitment and burning desire to confront the machinery of racism and anti-Semitism. And uppermost in Marc's mind was the thought that, "Possibly no other single point in the world has affected the whole of humankind as has Auschwitz." Dean wrote, "I'm most interested in meeting with the survivors in Israel, to see how these people have reintegrated themselves into society and how they have not let their experiences diminish their hope in humankind." Jonathan's words reflected his fear of indifference, "I can anticipate only feelings of sorrow because the Holocaust monuments probably mean nothing to the people living in Europe now."

"In a way," wrote Sue, "I almost feel guilty going to the camp as a free person. This guilt, however, makes me feel determination and it gives me a sense of mission to remind people of the Holocaust in order that it may never happen again . . . never to let our own hatred or resentment overcome us. We must be objective students with no personal animosity, for if we have hatred, we are defeating the very purpose for our journey."

Here are some answers to the second question: "What are your thoughts about entering the concentration camps?" Bob commented, "At first I'll probably feel apprehension about entering the gates because I sometimes have an irrational fear that time will turn back and I'll find myself in the 1940s when the camps were operating. As we walk through the camps I may feel somewhat haunted by the emptiness and silence of the camps." Bertha Lautman, a survivor of the Holocaust, who traveled with us wrote, "I always wanted to go back to Auschwitz as a free person."

We arrived in Prague, each of us with different thoughts and feelings about the personal journey of conscience that lay before us.

At the Ruzin airport there was a moment of panic when Amy's passport and visa were held back for no apparent reason. "Of course, we're not leaving," reassured Craig, as the adults tried to communicate with the officials. Even Bertha's fluent Czech didn't help. We all had to wait until a long line of travelers were processed before Amy's visa was pulled from beneath the pile of passports and pompously stamped. We were then nodded through the gate and welcomed to Prague by our Cedok guide.

Prague had once been home to Bertha Lautman. It was the majestic capital city of the homeland of her childhood. For the students Prague was a fairy-tale city, rich in ancient castles, churches, imposing bridges, cobblestone streets, and a winding river through the middle of the city. Prague had once been one of the oldest and most important Jewish communities in Europe. Jews have lived in Prague since the year 906, with the exception of a three-year exile in the mid-eighteenth century. Marc had prepared a research paper on the more than one thousand-year-old history of the Jews in Prague, describing religious, cultural, and intellectual achievements as well as Jewish social service organizations. Even in the prosperous Jewish communities of Bohemia there were needy persons who required help and care. The Jews of Prague had a Bikkur Holim society for the sick and a Hevra Kadisha for the burial of the dead, and they even had a Mehalke Tarn'golim, an organization which served chicken soup every Sabbath to the sick and the poor.

The most famous prayer books were published in Prague. Built in 1268, the Old-New Synagogue, still known as the *Alt-Neue Schul,* was the most famous synagogue in the city and the exclusive domain of the chief rabbis of Prague.

What we saw in Prague were the remnants of this once proud and flourishing Jewish community.

Ever sensitive to what might be a biased or prejudiced remark, Craig corrected the government guide as she took us through the state-owned Jewish Museum during our first day in Prague. Pointing to a Passover seder table and to a family Sabbath scene, the guide said, "This is an ancient Jewish custom, celebrated in the past, and not part of modern Jewish people." Craig was quick to remind her that these celebrations were very much alive today. In the museum there was also a treasury of Jewish ritual objects and artifacts. The guide informed us that the collections of silver Kiddush or wine goblets, the Torah pointers and breastplates, the ornate silver Torah crowns, the Havdalah spice boxes, and all that we saw in the glass cases had been sent to Prague by the Nazis from ravaged Jewish communities throughout Europe. The guide indicated that Hitler had ordered this collection to be preserved as memorabilia of a defunct religion and a *Judenrein* (free of Jews) Europe.

Towering over the former Jewish quarter on the right bank of the Moldau River is the Jewish clock. Its symbols are Hebrew letters which mark time just as it did when Maiselova Street was filled with devout Jews hurrying to synagogue for Friday night services. The Star of David still graces the sidewalk, and piercing the skyline is the crown of the Maisel Synagogue.

In the sanctuary of the Alt-Neue Synagogue we touched the bimah and chair of Rabbi Judah Loew ben Bezalel, the holy Maharal of Prague. He was the famous seventeenth-century scholarly rabbi who created the legendary Golem, the figure of clay which was to protect the Jews from evil. We had seen all of the artifacts and had visited the Jewish Museums, and most of what we had seen were the remains of a once vibrant Jewish life.

One question prevailed, "Where are the Jews?" Jon and Craig asked the guide, "What is left of Jewish life in Prague?" She took us outside to the cemetery. Nearby was the Pinkas Synagogue and on its walls were inscribed the names of the seventy-five thousand Jews from Bohemia and Moravia who perished in the Holocaust. The cemetery was strangely impressive. There were 12,000 gravestones, but we were informed that 95,000 people are buried there, so the dead must be buried at least eight deep in the ground since the headstones stand very closely together. As is customary, on the gravestones of some of the more famous people of the Jewish community in Prague, visitors had placed pebbles, candles, and slips of paper with messages and wishes on them as though they wanted to leave a personal memento behind.

Prague wasn't all somberness and death however. There were the emotional meetings with the elderly minyan for Sabbath services in the Alt-Neue Synagogue, the sharing of the sparse but tasty communal Sabbath meal of soup and gefilte fish, and the exciting walking tour to the fabled Hradcanske Castle. It was Craig who encouraged Mrs. Mann and Mrs. Rabinsky to come with him, Bob, and Sue across the bridge through old Prague and up the hundreds of steps to the magnificent walled church and castle. He thought we needed some emotional relief from the sad realities of our first day in Prague. We won't forget the picture of Craig, bundled in his knitted cap and scarf, standing alone on the heights overlooking the jeweled city, reflecting with us on what Sue had just said about the first day of our journey, "Today I was hit by the extent of the Holocaust. It's easy to sit in a classroom and discuss how Jewry was wiped out in Europe. Today, for the first time, we saw the remnants."

2

Lidice, a City Destroyed

Sound sleep in a feather bed did wonders for anyone suffering from fatigue after the long flight. By the second day in Prague, we were all anxious to begin our tightly packed itinerary. Ahead lay the unknown. No amount of classroom study or pre-trip seminars could have prepared the students for this morning.

Prague didn't remind anyone of Cleveland, Ohio! Here, the old buildings were lined up like so many pictures in a history book. The town square where we had shopped the day before seemed so unreal that it could just as well have been a movie set or a street straight out of Disneyland! The ornate buildings seemed like cardboard store fronts, so dusty and dilapidated and covered with centuries of grime and soot. Everything seemed grey, the buildings, the people, and the sky.

The first impressions of Prague had been recorded in the students' journals; they understood the importance of writing about each day before going to sleep at night. Those entries would be referred to later on to help them recall where and how the journey of conscience took shape and developed.

Their journals would also preserve images of people bundled up in heavy clothing, wearing boots, men in Russian-style fur hats, a few attractive women, but most solid and plain, cumbersome and unusual baby carriages, dingy streetcars rattling by, tall spires on ornate churches, worn pavements, careening cars coming pell-mell down curving streets, flights of steps separating levels of the city, the St. Charles Bridge spanning the river, flocks of birds overhead, the chiming of a church clock, serious soldiers standing guard, the intense cold at night and the empty streets.

Everyone was in a jovial mood as we gathered in the hotel dining room. Bob Somers loved the waiters' continental formality. He had awakened early and, like everyone else, was gulping down a breakfast of little rolls and sweet coffee. Bob's forte was his quick wit and way with words, and he enjoyed these moments of talking and joking with the other students. Many times in the days ahead, he was to highlight a particular moment with just the right words.

Bob was one of the most sensitive students on the trip. Although his home life was riddled with both emotional and financial troubles, he was determined to surmount these difficulties and do well in school. The prospect of scholarship money and independence at college was in the future. This trip was a stepping stone in that direction. Bob's happy face glowed with excitement at the prospect of this day. His zest for learning and eagerness to communicate what he was feeling gave him a special sparkle.

Outside the hotel, on a narrow, winding street a bus was waiting to take us on our first "field trip." We would be accompanied by an official government guide, stately Yolanda in her majestic white fur hat. (Her aloof manner gradually disappeared when she admitted that she herself was an underground Jew.)

Bob led the students onto the bus where the teachers were waiting to review facts about Lidice, their destination this morning. The small town was in a rural district northwest of Prague. It had been totally destroyed by the Nazis in 1943 and was rebuilt by survivors after the war.

Blue skies and a brilliant sun played upon the bright colors of the students' scarves, hats, and mittens. Everyone scrambled for seats near the windows as they prepared for the hour-and-a-half bus ride. Bob was enjoying himself immensely! He did feel twinges of uneasiness even though he was snug and warm. "Shouldn't we be more serious," he wondered, "considering our destination and mission? You'd think from the way everyone was acting that we were off on a picnic!" But try as he would, Bob couldn't summon any somber feelings to alter his good mood. As the Czech countryside flew past the bus windows, he thought about the irony of fate and about the Nazi whose assassination would be linked forever to the history of Lidice.

Reinhard Heydrich was one of Hitler's proteges and his rise to prominence in the Nazi party had brought him great power. Tall, blonde, and athletic in outward appearance, he was the very model of the Nordic type, the ideal Aryan—the German "superman." Inwardly, he was a villain. As head of the Reich Security Service and the first administrator of the concentration camps, he was a specialist in Nazi terror. His sadistic traits were recognized at the Wannsee Conference, a secret meeting held in a suburb of Berlin on January 20, 1942. Here, the plans for "The Final Solution" were confirmed, and Heydrich was chosen to execute the annihilation of the Jews by gas and by fire. However, his own death was to come suddenly just a few months later.

As Deputy Reich Protector of Bohemia and Moravia, Heydrich was responsible for all pacification measures in occupied Czechoslovakia. His methods were so brutal that widespread underground resistance ensued, and Czech exiles in London vowed to strike back. On May 27, 1942, three young men of the Czech Resistance were dropped by parachute in the vicinity of Prague. Two days later, on May 29, they waited for Heydrich's automobile at the edge of the city. As the car slowed down, one of them, Jan Kubis, threw a bomb that exploded under the vehicle. Heydrich was critically wounded and died a week later.

The reaction in Germany was bitter. An enraged Hitler looked upon Heydrich's assassination as a "lost battle," and in a funeral speech he eulogized Heydrich as the "Man with the Iron Heart." To retaliate for the murder, Hitler ordered that hundreds of Czechs be put to death in Prague. Because of a charge that the assassins had been harbored in the Christian village of Lidice, the Führer also decreed that the entire village be obliterated and its inhabitants executed or imprisoned.

As the bus approached the Lidice Peace Pavilion, Bob's attention was drawn to the severe pathway leading straight to the memorial. The pavilion itself was an open gazebo flanked on either side by enclosed breezeways leading to the center structure. Its high roof was secured by a circle of sturdy columns, and suspended from the ceiling was the Czech word *Mir*, "peace." Nearby stood the museum where the students would hear one survivor's personal story. Stretching in front of them was the winter remnant of a huge rose garden which had been planted in honor of the martyrs and paid for with pennies sent by children all over the world. In the distance was the rebuilt village of Lidice.

Inside the museum, the students clustered around a survivor who served as the museum guide. She was a small, stocky woman, slightly stooped, with ruddy cheeks and piercing eyes. Her head was covered with a vivid yellow wool stocking cap. In halting Czech, translated by Bertha Lautman and Yolanda, she told the group how, in retribution for Heydrich's murder, the Nazis had killed every village male over the age of fourteen. Pointing to the two hundred pictures, names, birthdates displayed on a wall, she said that her husband had been one of them. Near the pictures were marble plaques on which were inscribed the names of the men and women from Lidice who died in World War II. She ended by saying that she and the other women and children of the village had been sent to Ravensbruck Concentration Camp, where her infant daughter was killed.

During her explanation many questions raced through Bob's mind. "How can she tell this story over and over again? I would think her personal suffering would be too great." "What should *we* be saying to *her*?" he wondered. "Why was the new Lidice rebuilt adjacent to the old site and not *on* it?" he asked.

Patiently, the survivor went on, "Look in front of you as far as your eyes can see. At one time, you would have seen our village, bustling and alive. Now, there is only empty space. It is fitting that the village was not rebuilt on its original location, because it would be more difficult for a visiting world to grasp the totality of the destruction if it were covered by new buildings. The fact that the valley is totally empty except for the grass and trees underscores what remains—a cemetery. Return to your homes and your families, but remember the Martyrs of Lidice, remember us."

The students thanked her and walked silently to the bus. After this day in Lidice they were beginning to feel the emotional impact of their own personal encounter with the Holocaust. This journey of conscience was to become a turning point in their lives.

That night, Bob wrote in his journal, "Today, I had my first face-to-face encounter with Nazi atrocities. Lidice was a clear example of Nazi brutality. The Memorial and surrounding area were so extraordinarily silent that I felt my ears straining to hear some noise—any noise—but there was nothing. A sense of desolation and eeriness seemed to engulf the whole area. It's extremely difficult to believe that a whole town once stood there and now there is nothing."

3

No Names in Terezin

Lou was the first of our group to get married, and we never would have guessed it. We first met Chani, his bride to be, when she came to meet us at Kennedy Airport upon our return from Europe. She was a lovely, dark-haired and slender girl whom Lou smilingly introduced as, "My friend from the university." Lou never said much, but he was an achiever and an organizer.

Halfway through the semester of the first Holocaust class in Heights High, after having met with survivors and after having studied about Majdanek, Bergen-Belsen, Terezin, and Auschwitz, Lou remarked that what we were doing was not enough, so he organized the first Holocaust Outreach Program ever held in our city. Together with Craig, Marsha, Dean, Larry, and Sharon and with the help of twenty other students, Lou supervised and chaired the committee for "One Generation After," an ecumenical community forum to confront the events of the Holocaust.

Father Robert Bonnell, a Roman Catholic priest, known for his liberal opinions and social service activities participated in the forum. Father Bonnell had been on a mission to Israel and had visited Yad Vashem, the Memorial to the Six Million in Jerusalem. Father Bonnell told the audience of four hundred people that, in his years of study for a doctorate in contemporary history, he had never learned about the extent of the tragedies of the Holocaust Era. It was not until he stood in the Memorial Hall of Yad Vashem before the Eternal

Flame and above the buried urns of human ashes from the concentration camps, that he realized how urgent it is for us to remember. Indeed he said, "We must remember!"

Lou gave the concluding speech at the forum and he told the audience that he was the child of survivors, that his was the generation after the Holocaust, and that we must all consider ourselves survivors simply because we are alive today. Therefore, it is incumbent upon each one of us to remember actively enough to prevent another Holocaust from occurring.

Lou chanted the prayers at Terezin, the concentration camp where his own mother had been a prisoner. Our trip to Terezin, also known as Thereisenstadt, was made through a bitterly cold, yet sunny countryside, and was about an hour and a half from Lidice by bus. Prior to our journey we had studied about Terezin, known as the model camp, having been built like a small city with a quaint railroad depot, cultivated gardens, an outdoor cafe, a library, and an artists' workshop in the hope of convincing the International Red Cross of the liberal treatment of its prisoners. Terezin was the transit station to the death camps and fifteen thousand children had journeyed to this model camp. Of those children only one hundred survived. We had seen the drawings and read the poems of the children of Terezin in class. The haunting verse about the butterfly by Pavel Friedman will always live in our memories. Pavel was a child who was taken to Terezin in April 1942. He died in Auschwitz in September 1944.

The Butterfly

> The last, the very last,
> So richly, brightly, dazzlingly yellow
>> Perhaps if the sun's tears would sing
>> against a white stone.
>
> Such, such a yellow
> Is carried lightly 'way up high
> It went away I'm sure because it wished to
>> kiss the world goodbye.

For seven weeks I've lived in here,
Penned up inside this ghetto
But I have found my people here.
The dandelions call to me
And the white chestnut candles in the court.
Only I never saw another butterfly.

That butterfly was the last one.
Butterflies don't live here,
    In the ghetto.

Deeply moved by the children's paintings and poems, expressing sadness, homesickness, fear, and hope, our students responded with their own poetry and drawings in memory of the children. Lou wrote this poem.

Children of the Holocaust

CHILDREN
    Innocent flowers in bushes of thorns,
CHILDREN
    Millions dead for whom we mourn.
CHILDREN
    Their only sin being their religion.
CHILDREN
    Ending up as corpses of destruction.
HOLOCAUST
    In midst of destruction and doom,
HOLOCAUST
    A child is born from his mother's womb.
HOLOCAUST
    The child sees Nazis, Hitler, and genocide,

HOLOCAUST
Then is gassed by his father's side.
HOLOCAUST
Children killed for all generations.
CHILDREN
Who, to the last moment, hoped for salvation
HOLOCAUST
Has caused the tremendous loss, of the
CHILDREN
Of the Holocaust.

At the Terezin cemetery, overlooking the endless rows of unmarked gravestones, Lou intoned the Kaddish, the prayer for the dead, for the thousands whose ashes are buried there. We stood silently on that late afternoon, watching the sun as it carved oblique designs around the continuous stone slabs, realizing that this was the first time that we had faced the enormity of death and the anonymity of death.

About this Lou wrote, "The trip to Terezin was unbelievable. My mother had described it exactly the way it still is. The gravestones were an oddly touching memorial because they had no names on them. No names? No names? Everyone has a name. Don't you see? We shouldn't take our names for granted. To be without a name is to be without identity or even acknowledgement of death."

Terezin evoked strong feelings in most of the students. The town of Terezin was built as a fortress in the mid-eighteenth century by Emperor Joseph II of Austria. He named the massive star-shaped battlement after his mother, Maria Theresa. Although Terezin never really served as a fortress, it became, instead, a small army garrison town. The town is located about sixty kilometers from Prague.

During World War II the Nazis utilized Terezin, first as a ghetto, and then as the city of deception, the stopping place en route to the gas chambers.

Janet had this to say: "Terezin was an experience that I never thought I would have. So many thoughts occur at the same time. The fortress is so massive that it seems to represent the impregnability of the Nazi machine, even if it was built in 1760 or so. As I walked through the various parts of the camp one thought kept running through my mind, They're trying to kill me. They're trying to kill my people."

As we continued walking through the street of the camp and into the barracks, the truth about Terezin suddenly became startlingly real to us. Ronnie commented, "We walked around and then came to a sign reading, *Arbeit Macht Frei*, 'Work Makes You Free.' And it really struck me in a weird way. The only freedom that the work ever brought to most of the prisoners was death. But maybe death was better. At least death brought rest and peace instead of unbearable mental and physical torment." In his journal Ronnie wrote, "I was standing in the room next to what I thought was a gas chamber. Or was it really just a huge shower room? I was looking out the window and began to ask questions such as 'What did they think before they died? Did they think of their families, their own lives? Were they afraid or were they glad the torture would soon be over?' " "I wanted to capture the entire atmosphere," wrote Marc, "the stark rooms with the wooden bunks, the German words identifying the various rooms, and most of all the smell of death which lingers on and is engraved into the very walls." Walking around, some of us noticed a small cell which we entered. We remarked that the five of us really filled up that cell with no space to spare. We discovered a plaque in the room and asked Bertha to translate it. It said that eighty-five people had been punished and had been forced to stay in that same little cell where we stood. Kenny expressed his anger as he wrote, "The Nazis had to be machines to perpetrate these crimes against their fellow human beings."

"Jews from thirty-four nations were brought to Terezin and those who remained alive there could look forward to Auschwitz." Betsy added, "I am reminded of the prisons and jail houses of early America. But the cells at Terezin have no windows, only solid doors. And the prisoners must have slept three or four to one bunk."

Helplessness and futility were the emotions that some of us experienced. Dean wrote, "I did not feel a huge concern specifically for the Jews, but more for humankind in general. How can one person do this to another? I couldn't help but start crying at one point. I felt so helpless and upset. The Memorial to the Dead gave me an eerie feeling. It was as if the quiet of death hung over it. Everything was so still and icy cold." "As I was walking through Terezin and Lidice," noted Sarah, "I felt a sense of total despair. I completely lost my faith in mankind." Bob and Marc, recalling the children of Terezin, wrote in their journals, "Now we know how the children of Terezin felt when they wrote their poems"; "There were no butterflies in Terezin, only lice"; "We understand now why butterflies refused to visit Terezin."

For Bertha Lautman, the visit to Terezin was part of her journey back to revisit the terrors of her teen years. "At Terezin the barracks looked like the ones I remembered from Auschwitz. They gave me the shivers. I became very depressed. The one thing that they had here that I did not remember from Auschwitz was a huge barrel for washing lice-ridden clothes. We were unable to see the crematoriums since we did not have enough time and besides that, they were locked. I left with a very heavy heart. The mere physical place affected me, but the letters from the children affected me most of all. There is one letter in particular that will always remain with me. A child had written to her aunt saying, that she did not know where her parents were, and please to send some food and clothes since all she had was what was on her back."

* * * * * *

As we left Terezin, the sun was setting and Lou urged the bus driver to hurry so that we would be in Prague in time for Sabbath Eve services. There was no time to freshen up at the hotel as we rushed into the crowded small back annex of the Alte-Neue Synagogue. This is the oldest remaining synagogue in all of Europe and was built in 1270. The synagogue was then the center of a new settlement of Jews in Prague, many of whom had come from Germany. It has great historic significance, because through the centuries, despite the periodic upheavals in the Jewish community, the plague in the late seventeenth century, the persecutions in the mid-eighteenth century, Jews continued to pray in the Alte-Neue Synagogue.

On Friday night, we joined in prayer with twenty-one elderly men, the remnants of the former Jewish community of Prague. The members of the small congregation were amazed to see our motley crew of students and teachers. When Lou and Jon joined in the Hebrew prayers and even chanted the songs, some of the elderly men cried. One gentleman, who later introduced himself in good English to us, said that they would never believe that young American Jews were still practicing the traditions. To most of us, however, the congregation, barely more than a minyan, was proof of the extent of the Holocaust. Sue wrote, "I cannot imagine what keeps these people in Prague. As I left the synagogue I began imagining the street forty years ago: the excitement of hurrying to services, the smell of freshly baked challah, the voices of the cantors echoing out into the street from the seven synagogues."

We had a Sabbath dinner in the Jewish Town Hall or community center which is just a few feet away from the Alte-Neue Synagogue. Some twenty or thirty Jews and guests gather each week for a communal kosher and festive Sabbath meal on Friday night and Saturday noon. Kosher meat is brought in from Bratislava. The services and the Sabbath meal are the only tangible expressions of Judaism here. What was surprising to us was that all of the cooking was done by Aunt Magda, Bertha and Michael Lautman's aunt-by-marriage. The food was tasty and warm, even though it wasn't sumptuous. "This week there is meat for Saturday, only. It is too expensive to have meat twice," said Aunt Magda. Dean appreciated the communal get-together. He wrote, "Shabbat dinner in the small kosher kitchen next door to the synagogue was typically Jewish. We had a type of gelfilte fish, challah, a huge bowl of chicken noodle soup (of course) for a main dish and some type of strudel for dessert. The atmosphere was so warm and congenial—the first I've encountered since being here."

Other surprises during the dinner greeted Mrs. Rabinsky. During the meal many of the congregants came up and asked, "Where were you born? Do you come originally from Europe? Were your parents from Europe?" Casually, Mrs. Rabinsky answered that her parents came from Czechoslovakia, but that prior to World War I they came from Hungary. "My father came from Ungvar, and my mother from Novo-Mesto." "Novo Mesto," cried out the man who had been the cantor, "why, here we have Novo Mesto." He proceeded to introduce Mrs. Rabinsky and the group to the elderly, stately man who had chanted the Sabbath kiddush over the wine. "This is our community leader, Dr. Paul Gruenfeld. He is from Novo Mesto, too." Dr. Gruenfeld warmly inquired who Mrs. Rabinsky's family was. Her grandfather, a rabbinical and secular scholar, had been the Orthodox rabbi of Novo Mesto and the dean of a yeshiva, a Talmudic studies seminary. "Herr Dr. Rabiner Rosenberg," exclaimed Dr. Gruenfeld, "of course, of course! His son, Sandor, (Mrs. Rabinsky's uncle, also a rabbi) was my closest friend! Are you really from the Herr Rabiner's family?" There was a tearful and warm embrace, as all of the students crowded around. Marc, ever alert, snapped a picture. "Come and meet someone else from Novo Mesto," said Dr. Gruenfeld. He brought the students to a dignified, elegant woman and introduced her as Mrs. Yolann Strauss. She, too, became excited and emotional when she learned who Mrs. Rabinsky's relatives were. "Sari, Ciri, Rosi," she proceeded to name the children of the Rosenberg family. She remembered most of the seven who had been born in Novo Mesto. "We had the kosher restaurant in the city. Your grandfather gave the rabbinical supervision." "Why, I remember," said Mrs. Strauss, "when the rabbi left for America in 1921. My parents and I joined the entire Jewish community which went to the railroad station to wish him Godspeed." Mrs. Strauss maintains her ties with the past through the community Shabbat dinner on Friday night.

Overwhelmed with emotion, Mrs. Rabinsky spoke with Dr. Gruenfeld and Mrs. Strauss in halting German and some Yiddish. She later told the group, "I came to Prague and among the remnants I found my roots."

The first few days in Prague left many other indelible memories. We will never forget Lou's beastly toothache, a wisdom tooth dragon, cutting a thousand sharp fangs through his sensitive swollen gums, and it hurt. Bertha and Mrs. Rabinsky had to take Lou to an all-night dental clinic by cab. God bless Bertha. She is winsome, charming, and has a way with people, especially the Prague people. And she speaks Czech. Lou was helped with medication (he refused to have the tooth pulled) and by morning, he was better.

For Ron, there was pain of another kind, the pain of having lost grandparents and so many relatives. Visiting Prague was especially meaningful for Ron. "This was my father's home country," remarked Ron. "So much of my father's life is a mystery to me. Coming here helped me understand a little of his life, but there is still so much more to know." Ronnie had joined Marc and Dean in wandering through the maze of streets with closely-stacked buildings, many of them with identification marks, such as roses or faces, which had been etched in the Middle Ages. Dean wrote that he will always remember the tower with the clock where statues of the Apostles announced each hour and the walk along the Moldau River and across the St. Charles's Bridge.

Sue, too, was fascinated by the beauty of Prague. Yet, she was puzzled. "It's hard to believe that a city as lovely as Prague could ever have been confronted with World War II," she wrote. "I wonder where the Czech men I have seen were during the war. During the past three days I have felt the impact of the Holocaust like never before. Europe's once large Jewish population is indeed gone."

Sarah's most vivid impression in Prague was of St. Jacob's, an Eastern Orthodox church, hundreds of years old. "St. Jacob, what a beautiful name. Today I felt closer to God than I have ever felt in my life," she wrote. "The minute I walked into the cathedral, I felt a warmth in my body and I fell to my knees and prayed. Tears were coming down my face. I could have stayed in the church for hours, even days, except that I felt that the group was waiting for me." Sarah and Betsy went back to St. Jacob's later on Saturday. Betsy had spoken about the elaborate frescoes on the ceiling, the six or eight altars for patron saints, the gorgeous chancel, and "the best pipe organ in Europe." They were upset that the church was not open. In her journal Sarah wrote, "I wanted to give thanks for what I have experienced and I believe that we are going to need God every step of the way. I realize that I can pray in my room, but I feel closer to God when I am in church. I know that we will all make it through this journey because God is with us and he will protect us."

4

Twelve Hours to Warsaw

This was the third day of our journey. It was a Saturday—the Sabbath. After sundown, our bus ride to Poland began. Dean looked eagerly forward to his twenty-first birthday and wondered what it would be like to celebrate this day in Poland, the country where his father was born and had grown up and where so many of the Stein relatives had been killed.

The tedious twelve-and-a-half-hour bus ride from Czechoslovakia into Poland seemed like a good time to catch up on sleep. Everyone complained about being tired! "I'll doze on the bus," Dean promised.

He looked at his watch and noted that it got dark early in Eastern Europe in December. He could just as well be looking out of a bus window back in Ohio, except that he knew that this countryside had a notorious past: the Nazis had probably used this very road when they moved in to batter and conquer Poland. Deportations in cattle cars bound for the concentration camps might have taken place on the railroad tracks running parallel to this route.

Dean had stomach cramps and he felt uneasy. "Am I sick for coming here?" he asked himself. "Why am I doing this? My father and his family fled from here in terror, and I'm sitting on a bus, counting the hours until we arrive in Poland."

The thought was frightening to him. He wondered if he should feel sadness because of the personal loss of relatives whom he had never known. It seemed so important to find a reason why he was here.

31

He thought he would give anything for a hot shower and a change of clean clothes. But that was impossible! Since noon the group's baggage had been sitting in one room waiting to be put on the bus. He probably wouldn't see his suitcase until he was in the lobby of the hotel in Warsaw.

Dean turned around and made a quick survey of the bus and discovered that Mrs. Rabinsky was curled up on the seat behind him. She was trying to sleep off a migraine headache. Usually she had so much pep and was a step ahead of everyone. He supposed it was tension. They weren't exactly on a pleasure trip. Besides, she also had to cope with schedules, arrangements, and all the other problems. He marveled that everything was going smoothly so far.

The singing and usual loud chatter on the bus had quieted down. Dean had not relaxed. Some of the students were clustered around Bertha Lautman and others, sitting two by two, were quietly exchanging thoughts. Dean closed his eyes.

It was after midnight when the students were jolted awake by an abrupt stop. "Where are we?" "Some rest stop!" "Pizza time." "How long will we be here?" Everyone came alive. Beyond the bus was an area flooded with light revealing a barrier across the road. A guard station nearby was veiled by falling snow. Suddenly, the bus door swung open and two border guards jumped in and faced the students. "You have arrived at the Czechoslovakian-Polish border," they announced in broken English. "You must leave all Czech money inside the country. You will not be allowed to take any Czech currency across the border. You must declare how much each of you have. The Czechoslovakian-Socialist Republic will send your money to you. It is a crime to carry money across the border."

The soldiers' stern faces and brusque manner convinced everyone that they meant business. A few tried to make jokes to cover up their fears, but Dean knew that they were as frightened as he was. Soon everyone became busy searching for Czech coins! This night, no one wanted to take a chance.

Leafing through the passports that had been handed to him, one of the guards began shouting out names, asking the students to identify themselves. What's going on, Dean wondered. How do people get used to this treatment or are these soldiers hassling us just because we're foreigners? Whatever it was, he was uncomfortable, and wished he knew what was going on.

Hours passed, and the students shivered on the bus as they waited for Mrs. Mann and Mrs. Lautman to come back from the guard shelter. The two women had been given innumerable official papers and forms to sign.

Dean was irritated. He was one of the students who had advised exchanging the money at the airport that afternoon. But no one had wanted to lose those precious leisure hours in Prague. So now they were being held up. "It's good that we figured our money so closely," Dean thought. "Who knows if we will ever get any of it back?"

As the bus began to move, Dean suddenly realized that they were, indeed, a long, long way from home.

In the early hours of the morning, as they arrived in the city, Warsaw looked more like an American city waking up to go to work than any place Dean had seen thus far. As the bus pulled up in front of the modern Grand Orbis Hotel, the students groaned. Exhausted from the all-night ride they knew they would have to begin unloading suitcases, waiting for room assignments, unpacking and, this afternoon, finally begin to travel the route of the Warsaw Ghetto.

Dean thought he would never complain again about a full work load at school. "What was hard about going to classes and studying?" he wondered, as he staggered off the bus and took his place in line to heave suitcases onto the sidewalk.

"What next?" chorused the students when the hotel manager informed them that their rooms weren't ready. "We can squeeze into two small rooms for the time being," Mrs. Rabinsky said. "While everyone rests, Bertha and I will go with the bell boy to the local flower shop. We need a wreath for our first presentation at the Warsaw Ghetto."

5

The Warsaw Ghetto

Snow began to fall in the gloom of the late afternoon. Despite efforts to rouse one another, nobody seemed able to get up enough energy or enthusiasm for sightseeing. It would be so wonderful to go back to the hotel, take off the cold boots and damp socks, find a warm blanket and curl up at a fireside. But no! The teachers insisted on using every last moment of the day. "When," they asked, "would the group have this opportunity again?"

Scott Baskin wanted to answer, "Never and who cares?" But he knew that he *did* care and so did all of the students. They were just *so* tired. Making the commitment to go on this journey meant giving up the winter break at home to travel thousands of miles retracing the path of the Holocaust. The choice has been my own, Scott thought to himself.

In the afternoon the group boarded a bus for Pawiak Prison. Ray, the smooth-talking guide from the Polish travel agency, had explained that once political prisoners were housed there.

Scott thought about the gamut of crimes that the label "political prisoner" could cover. As the students walked through the underground dungeon, Scott was overcome by its morbid atmosphere. He tried to imagine living through years of imprisonment, but he couldn't believe that any prisoner was strong enough to outlast a sentence at Pawiak. In the central souvenir area (the students were finding souvenirs in all the buildings open to the

35

public!) was a model of the entire prison compound and the group lingered there, listening to Ray's explanation. It was almost dark outside when they again boarded the bus. The teachers were determined to travel the route of the Warsaw Ghetto.

Scott knew that he was expected to place a wreath at the ghetto Memorial and say something about the group's purpose for coming. He had thought about this. He had written the words down on paper, shared his thoughts with Mrs. Rabinsky, but he still wasn't satisfied. Back home at Ohio State Scott was never at a loss for words. He usually exuded self-confidence, and he hoped that his flair for rhetoric would help him out now.

Scott Baskin's family had traveled extensively and their holiday excursions had introduced them to places all over the United States, but this was Scott's first trip to Europe. Some of the students envied his travel experience, but here, as they approached the first street corners of the ghetto area, he felt as green as the rest of them.

Each student was given a map that outlined the Warsaw Ghetto. The names of the streets familiar from their studies were now right in front of them: Mila, Krochmalna, Nowolipie.

The students marked their maps to correspond with the turns and curves of the bus. This was unforgettable territory. It was here in November of 1940 that half a million Jews were shoved and contained behind walls. Access to and from the area was only through guarded gates, and few were allowed passage except to work in forced labor camps. Little did the victims dream that their fate was sealed behind these walls and that the Nazis would soon begin the diabolically planned mass extermination of the Jews. Haphazardly crowded into a space that was meant to house 35,000 people, isolated and restricted, the ghetto residents were denied the necessities of everyday life. Food, clothing, shelter, education, means of a livelihood—all of these were gradually taken away by the Nazis until the Jews were forced to survive on the barest of rations and under the most perverse conditions. Huge numbers died daily from starvation and disease. A welfare report published in 1942 summarized the situation: "Sickness, hunger, and want are the constant companions of the refugees of the ghetto and death is the only visitor in their homes."

Mrs. Mann turned to the guide. Outraged, she questioned where the Polish residents of the surrounding area had been during this period. "Ray, you must have been a teenager while this was going on. Where was everybody? Why didn't your parents respond to this injustice?"

"We didn't know," Ray said. "The Jews were forced to post large signs reading, *Danger: Epidemic Zone, Typhoid Beware.* The Nazis fooled us into believing that the ghetto was built to protect us. How were we to know it wasn't true?"

Betsy Jenkins, the shy daughter of a Christian clergyman, was sitting in the back of the bus. She could keep silent no longer. "Excuses! Excuses! That's what we learned about in class. When there was still time to save the Jews, even before the war started, no one cared. Every nation had an excuse for not taking in the unfortunate refugees. At the beginning, Hitler had no plans for annihilation. All he wanted was to make Germany *Judenrein*, 'cleansed of Jews.' But when no nation offered strong protest or offered to help, the Nazis interpreted this as a mandate to do the job thoroughly. The whole world, the apathetic world, is to blame for what happened in the death camps."

Scott joined in. "What about all the Warsaw residents who should have hated the Nazis for what they did to Poland? What did they do beside turn their backs on the helpless people in the ghetto? They probably thought 'Why look at something unpleasant? Maybe if we deny what's happening it'll be easier to forget the Jews behind those walls.' "

"It just makes me sick," Betsy cried. "Sick and disgusted."

Ray looked at her and said quietly. "I know how you feel but that's the way it was."

Just ahead of the bus was the *Umschlagplatz*, the central depot where the deportees were brought before they were sent to the death camps. Quotas were sent by the Nazis each day and the SS was merciless in seeing that these were fulfilled. People of all ages and positions were brought here; they were taken out of their beds, from off the streets, summoned by official decree. Active resistance was impossible. The Nazi clubs and guns silenced all protest.

The students tried to visualize the frenzied agony that must have taken place here, amidst kisses, reassuring words between loved ones and friends. How many families were separated here? How many last goodbyes were said? What remained beside ghostly memories? The students saw that the Umschlagplatz had been turned into a parking lot.

They traveled on to Memorial Square, officially renamed Ghetto Fighter's Square. In the center was sculptor Nathan Rapaport's statue of Mordecai Anielewicz, the twenty-three-year-old leader of the Warsaw Ghetto Uprising. The monument had two sides: Anielewicz, defender of the ghetto on the front, and a procession of ghetto dwellers on the back. Stooped and broken, they represented the tormented Jewish people whose act of survival was also a form of resistance.

The monument paid tribute to all those inhabitants of the ghetto who, despite the pain and suffering of Nazi persecution, never lost the will to live and hope for the future, a future which for most of them meant death.

Scott was to make the presentation in front of the monument. He hoped to speak for all of the students. This monument was more than a slab of granite; he had to convey that somehow.

For Scott, the moment took on a sharp clarity. His eyes took in everything around him: the strength of Anielewicz's defiant figure standing before them in strong silence, the falling snow blown by the biting wind, the students standing in quiet groups waiting to hear him, their bodies huddled together for warmth, the detachment of the Polish children, just a few feet away, oblivious to the monument and probably to what it represented. He saw street lights ringing the open plaza in which they stood. Beyond the fringe of light, high-rise apartments towered against the sky. Scott wondered if the residents on the upper floors had any thoughts about their view.

This is what he said, "What is an uprising? Is it a defense against inhuman oppression or is it an offensive to prolong the chance of survival? For the inhabitants of the Warsaw Ghetto, it was both. We, of the Journey of Conscience, dedicate this wreath in solemn remembrance of the defenders of the Warsaw Ghetto. Hear us, valiant people who lived, fought and died here. We remember."

A short ride away was Mila 18. Here the leaders of the uprising had established headquarters in a bunker beneath the street and from here, they directed the defense of the ghetto.

It was on Passover Eve 1943 that a German force, equipped with tanks and artillery, penetrated into the ghetto but met with stiff resistance from the Jewish fighters. The defenders were outnumbered, their arsenal of a few smuggled and homemade weapons was pitiful. Yet, they were fortified by the fierce desire to die with dignity.

A second commander, General Jürgen Stroop, led a new attack. This time, the Nazis did not engage in open street combat. Instead, they systematically began to burn down houses. The inhabitants died in the flames while those hiding in the bunkers were killed by gas and hand grenades. Despite these conditions, the Jewish fighting groups continued to attack German soldiers. They held off the Nazi onslaught for forty-three days.

In Mila 18, Anielewicz lost the battle and his life, but he won a spiritual victory no weapon could ever crush.

"Does the world know this story?" Kenny Myers wondered. "The defenders of the ghetto were so proud, so determined to resist and beat the odds they faced. And yet, what they did seems to have been forgotten."

Lou agreed and sarcastically said, "Let it be known that there was no Warsaw Ghetto or Warsaw Revolt—there wasn't one if you have never heard or studied about it because if you go to the place where the ghetto stood, you will find nothing but the monument and a mound of earth marking Mila 18."

Mrs. Rabinsky could sense the students' anger and frustration, but felt confident that their deep emotions at this moment would be translated into positive efforts. Certain that her students' feelings and reactions not only conveyed what they had learned, but also demonstrated the values that have true meaning—compassion, understanding, and wisdom, she watched as they walked slowly around the bunker. Ronnie stood alone, contemplative. Scott, riveted to the spot, had tears in his eyes. Marc was reading a passage from fighter Zivia Lubetkin's diary, while Ken, Lou, and Jon were listening and taking pictures. What remains? Who remembers? Mrs. Rabinsky silently blessed her students because she knew that they would carry on the responsibility of teaching the lessons of the Holocaust.

That night, Sarah wrote in her journal: "I really fell apart today. I think some of it was the fact that I had no sleep for the past thirty-two hours, but the Warsaw Ghetto monument really hit me. I gave part of the dedication speech and I cried like a baby. I suddenly wondered how the world could stand by and watch it happen. I felt a great hatred for anyone who collaborated with the Nazis. I just can't hold it in any more."

And a month later, Dean recalled this day for his grandparents. They reminded him of their past. "Do you remember, Dean, that we told you about our wedding in Warsaw sixty years ago? Our wedding night was spent in a suite of the apartment house at Mila 18."

Dean's response was stunned silence. Later, he admitted, "This, more than anything else, really blew my mind."

6

Bertha Lautman, Our Survivor

Farewells are very difficult for Bertha Lautman, even if the parting is for a joyous occasion. Just recently, Bertha's married son, Donnie, and his wife of two years, Ariela, left America to settle on a *kibbutz*, a collective farm, near Tel Aviv in Israel. After Donnie had graduated from high school, he had volunteered to go with his youth group for a year's stay on a kibbutz, in a work-study program. Donnie loved his work with the dairy herd. He became an expert on feeding and milking procedures. He even helped in the calving of the cows. The robust outdoor work,the cameraderie of the young volunteers, the warmth and idealism of the *vatikim*, "older settlers," and their program of religious traditions, work, and sharing appealed to seventeen-year-old Donnie. He was determined that one day, after his years of college training, he would find a young girl who would love to share this kind of life with him. They would come to Israel on *aliya*, a "going up" to settle on the land.

The time had come. Donnie and Ariela had both completed their masters' degrees in social work and both were anxious to live out their dreams and go to Israel. But Bertha was not ready for this separation. For the thirty-two years of their marriage, Bertha and Michael Lautman had been determined to raise a closely-knit family, where parents and children would share everything together, the triumphs and sadnesses, the joy of holiday celebrations, the achievements of schooling, the questions of career, the enrichment of happy marriages, the blessings of grandchildren. For Mike, life in America, his marriage to Bertha, his three children, and two grandchildren were a re-creation of life, a redemption from all that had been wrenched from him before. Mike was one of the *shearit hap'leta*, "the saving remnant." He was the only survivor of an entire family which had perished during the Holocaust.

Bertha was totally devoted to her family. She knew what it meant to grow up without a father and mother during the crucial teen years. She knew what it meant to be the youngest in a family of seven children and to be forcibly separated from one's brothers and sisters, not knowing for years whether any one in the family was still alive. Even though her own children, Jeffrey and Donnie, had been in college out of town, even though Alice, her daughter, had married and settled in New York, they were only a phone call away. Bertha and her children spoke to each other often and they were always together for vacations and holiday celebrations. Moving to Israel was different. It was so far away and so at Donnie's and Ariela's farewell party, Bertha cried.

She wept in class, also, when she came and told us about the separation from her own father and mother in March 1942. Bertha came to Room 300, immaculate in her white uniform (she is in charge of the occupational therapy department at a local home for the aged), and rather nervous. She asked for a glass of water before she sat down at a desk, joining the large circle of students. This was not the first time she had told her story to a Holocaust studies class, but each time was a trial for her, a dredging of her memories and emotions.

"It's never easy for me to talk about my past," Bertha began, "and this time of the year, it's even worse. It was during the month of March that I arrived at Auschwitz, four weeks before the Passover holidays. When we are so close to the holidays, I remember even more vividly than usual. The older I get, the worse it gets. Time really has not healed. You may wonder why I have come to speak to you about the Holocaust. Not too many survivors want to talk about their experiences, nor are they even able to talk about what happened to them. Mrs. Rabinsky asked me to come to class and although at first I didn't want to come, I am now grateful I did. I see how important it is for young people to know what happened during the Holocaust Era."

Bertha took some water, closed her eyes for a moment, and began to transport us back to her hometown in Czechoslovakia more than thirty-five years ago. "In 1940, I remember, we couldn't go to school anymore. Ever since 1938, when the Nazis came into Czechoslovakia, school was a waste of time for us. The Jewish children weren't tested. We were automatically given the worst grades. Nobody paid any attention to us. Toward the end of the school year, we were mistreated. I remember one teacher who was extremely mean. He even abused us physically.

"In 1940, when we had to leave school, we were ordered to wear the Star of David on our clothing. The businesses were taken away from the Jews. My father had a good business, a lumber yard, until the Nazis took it from him."

"It was in 1942 that I was taken away from home. It was strange how this came about," Bertha continued.

The students were unusually quiet. It often takes them ten to fifteen minutes to settle in, to forget a good story, before they can focus on their studies. With Bertha in class, all of the students were raptly attentive immediately. Her story brought reality to what they had read and to what they had heard.

"In 1942, a law came out that they would take girls first, from sixteen years of age. Where to? Of course, nobody knew. I wasn't of age, but my older sisters were hidden because we knew that they would be taken. When the police came and they didn't find my sisters, they wanted to take my father. It was inconceivable to me that my father would go and I would stay at home. So, I went. Do you know what it means to be taken from Father and Mother?" Bertha found it difficult to talk and searched for a tissue in her pocket, found one on the teacher's desk, sipped some water, but still had to stop for a moment. Her next sentences were halting as she wiped the tears from her eyes while she spoke. "Leaving home, as a young child, the youngest of seven children, leaving a very warm, closely-knit family wasn't easy. I can still feel my father's hands on my head as he blessed me. It is Jewish tradition that a father blesses his child. My mother came with me to the next city where Jews from East Slovakia were gathered, and from there I was taken, still with my mother, to yet another point where Jews from all over Slovakia were assembled. This was the city of Poprat and this is where I had to bid good-bye to my mother. Remember, this wasn't going to camp to get away from it all." The students smiled. Some even laughed, maybe to break the tension. "It was going to the unknown," said Bertha very quietly. "Little did I know that this would be the last time that I was to see my parents."

"The real journey now began," continued Bertha. "In Poprat we were all put on trains, cattle cars, packed like sardines. When I say packed, I mean packed. We traveled for two days and three nights, which seemed like years. How does one survive? I don't know. We had food because Mother had packed food, but there was no water, no washrooms. I really can't tell you how I survived. Wherever we would stop we would shout, 'Where are we? Where are we going?' People in the stations couldn't shout the answers. They didn't know where we were going. At one station closer to Auschwitz, people hollered, 'Maybe to Auschwitz.' Of course, we didn't know what Auschwitz was. We arrived at Auschwitz, March 23, 1942."

Some of the students began to turn around, looking at each other. We had all seen two very graphic, searing films, *Night and Fog* and *Memorandum*, both of which had shown actual scenes of Auschwitz and its victims, films taken by the Nazis. Now, Bertha Lautman would tell of what she, herself, had experienced there.

"The doors of the cattle car opened and what we saw were SS guards (the elite Nazi divisions, trained especially to deal with the concentration camps and their prisoners) and huge German Shepherd dogs. '*Raus! Raus! March schnell!* Out! Out! Hurry up!' Take luggage or don't take luggage. It didn't matter. But we did take whatever we were able to and we marched up to the camp. We were taken to the left for undressing. Now for a young girl, and it wasn't only me, but for most of us who came from a very religious background, to undress in front of men wasn't easy. We started to undress little by little, one piece at a time, but everything had to come off. Then we were made to go through three bathtubs. The first fifty girls were internally checked, tattooed, and marched up to the block. I was among the first fifty." Here Bertha turned her arm and raised it so that the students could see the blue tattoo mark on her forearm, still clearly visible. "This was my number and my name, 1048. I was never called by my real name after that, only by my number. You should know that the first thousand numbers were given to Christian Polish women who were among the first prisoners of Auschwitz. We were the first transport of Jewish girls."

"We were put in Block One where we remained four weeks without work. Every morning before four o'clock, our block would have to gather outside the building for *Appell*, 'the countings.' We stood in rows, three in a row, and they would count and count and count, sometimes for more than two hours, and it was freezing. Poland in March is still terribly cold."

Lou was to write later during our visit to Auschwitz, "This must have been the hell that froze over. It was cold, so cold that I was shivering through my winter clothes. And then I stopped, for I saw before my eyes people with almost no clothes on. I then became hot, hot with fear, with anger at myself for wearing these luxuries, with shame for not having been able to help these people in any way." Betsy, too, would feel the piercing wind of Auschwitz. "I do not understand how Mrs. Lautman and other survivors could withstand or tolerate the cold. The weather at Auschwitz and Birkenau was bitter and biting. We were freezing in our heavy winter coats and long underwear, sweaters, hats, scarves, and mittens. We could, and I did, look forward to going back to a nice warm bus, a warm hotel room and bed. Thirty years ago, the prisoners at Auschwitz and Birkenau had to endure that cold, with no relief, for days, months, years, all the time. I don't know how they did it. I really don't."

"Yes," said Bertha, "we were freezing and hungry and lonely. For four weeks we lay around during the day and talked. Our conversation was mostly about our parents. We were ready to give our lives just to see our parents once more." Bertha cried quietly and we sat in awesome silence. "You know what, I'm still ready," she added. "We also talked about food all of the time. After four weeks we were marched out to work. Again, *Appell*, marching out of the camp and then, digging ditches. I don't know what we were digging.

We just dug. At Auschwitz, and even later in Birkenau, we dug ditches. Then, marching back, *Appell*, and back to the barracks. Our food consisted of black coffee, if you could call it coffee, and a piece of bread. Sometimes at noon we had a kind of soup that was made from horse meat. But in the morning and evening, we had only black coffee and bread. All of this went on from March 1942 until August of that year. We were then taken to Birkenau, which was only five kilometers away. Birkenau was even worse than Auschwitz."

Our students had learned about Birkenau, the camp especially constructed for death, the camp where the railroad tracks emptied on to the ramps, where the people from the transports were divided into groups. The aged, the infirm, and the children all went to their deaths in the gas chambers, and the young and more able went to the labor battalions, a temporary respite from death. Craig wrote of his impression of Birkenau: "The appearance of the train station facade through the fog was mystical. It seemed to loom out of the darkness. The platform was incredibly long, at least three or four kilometers. It receded from the monument back through time to the station building. The whole atmosphere, with the fog, made the arrival of the transports all the more real. The selection ramp to Birkenau was worn from footsteps. Endless miles of barbed wire. From the platform, all we saw were rows upon rows of barbed wire, with guard towers every seventy-five yards or so, and the impenetrable fence. Birkenau represents the best evidence of Nazi intents and motives for Jewish genocide." Jon's journal entry after Birkenau revealed his wrath: "If my tears were that of anger, it was for the apathetic world that acknowledged the Nazis' plan by keeping silent. This day has made me realize that I will never allow myself to become apathetic. I have also found a peace of mind, knowing that after feeling a sorrow like I did today, I will never be part of a silent world, like that of the 1940s. I will fight physically or verbally if I believe an injustice has occurred."

Bertha continued to tell the class of her personal fight for survival. "In Birkenau, it was already fall and very cold. We were six prisoners to one bunk. They were bunk beds, but nothing like what you have in mind. We were sleeping on wood. It was freezing. I have always been a very cold person and I was afraid of the winter and of marching out.

So one day I heard that they were looking for girls to be in *Leichen Kommando*. This is the group that notices wherever there are corpses in the camp. The girls picked up the dead bodies and brought them to a *Leichen Halle*, a special booth for the bodies. The trucks would come at two o'clock in the morning and we would throw the corpses on the truck which took them to the crematorium. So what was so good about *Leichen Kommando*? I didn't have to stand *Appell*, my food was double, and we also had permission from the SS doctor to open the water once a day to wash our hands. This was a great thing.

"The girls that I came with, those whom my mother had told to watch over me, said, 'No, don't do that kind of work!' But, when I left my mother, I grew up instantly. I didn't listen to anyone and I got in to this group. The *Leichen Kommando* was terrible work, but it saved my life. We also got gloves to work with. I was in this work for thirteen months, day in and day out, throwing the corpses on the truck at two in the morning. Do you know what that means? I must tell you, though, that if we found the body of a girl we knew, we handled her very gently, saying the Kaddish or Memorial Prayer and asking her forgiveness for what we were doing. We then placed her body carefully on the truck."

"I had additional good fortune," said Bertha. "Good fortune," muttered one of the girls in the class. "There was a Slovak lady doctor and I was like her pet. She told me that thirteen months in this work was enough. So she put me in another Kommando, *Rote Kapchen* or 'red hats' because we wore red babushkas when we worked. Our job was to work with the belongings of the new arrivals. Many of them brought along food and we were able to eat it. So that wasn't a bad place to work either. We had to sort the luggage and clothing because the Nazis made use of everything. Sometimes you were able to put a sweater on under your uniform, and, if you were lucky marching back, the SS didn't check you."

"Well, I wasn't lucky enough. The very first day I twisted my ankle and I was positive that I was going to be taken straight to the crematorium. But I guess it was meant for me to survive. The following week I wanted to bring a blouse back for my friend, so I put it on under my uniform. The guards caught me with it and the first thing they did was to cut off my hair." Bertha stopped and we all watched as she touched the curls near her face. "That was the seventh time I had my head shaven."

During our journey to Auschwitz we saw the ceiling-to-floor wall of hair, mottled grey and dusty brown with age and the rolls of haircloth made from human hair. Scott wrote, "God! Mountains of hair taken from victims! How can men do things like this to other people? Unbelievable!" Bertha commented, "My hair, too, must be here."

Having her head shaven was the most dehumanizing experience for Bertha. She told the students of her utter depression after this punishment. "That was the only time I thought of committing suicide. To commit suicide in Auschwitz was very easy because we were surrounded by electrified barbed wire fences. You just touched a wire and that was it. I took away the bodies of many girls who died like that. I was lucky, once again, because I had a friend who talked me out of it. I never again thought of committing suicide because I lived on the hope of seeing my parents again."

Jay wrote about the barbed wire fence in Auschwitz, "I realize now that if people threw themselves against the electrical fence, they were saving room in the gas chamber for other people. I cannot blame them for committing suicide, because I do not know what I would have done, but it was like doing the Nazis a favor."

Bertha Lautman left Auschwitz-Birkenau on October 31, 1944. "To live through 1944 in Auschwitz, to see how fast they brought people in and how quickly they put them into the crematorium was unreal. The trains would come in one after the other. By the time the next train came, the first group of people were already gassed. The camp was lit up day and night from the crematoriums which were not too far from the camp in Birkenau. We could hear people scream *Sh'ma Yisroel,* 'Hear O Israel the Lord Our God, the Lord is One,' and the cries of the children. It was all very close. Unbelievable! It was strange, though, how I was able to leave Auschwitz and Birkenau."

"A friend of mine told me that Auschwitz would be liquidated completely and that if I had a chance to leave, I should go. How would I know where to go or what would be waiting for me? It was the unknown. A transport of girls was being taken to Bergen-Belsen, so I managed to be taken with them." Bergen-Belsen was another infamous concentration camp. Located in Germany, it was the camp to which Anne Frank was taken and where she died in 1945, shortly before the end of the war.

"Remember," continued Bertha, "This was almost at the end of 1944. There was very little food in Bergen-Belsen. We didn't work, the will was gone. Often we didn't even have the strength to come out and stand '*Appell*.' But somehow or other we went on. Another transport arrived again from Auschwitz and someone told me that my sister was in it. By this time I was used to being hungry, but I knew that my sister had just come to camp. I wanted to be able to help her if she would come to Bergen-Belsen, so I volunteered to work in the hospital. This meant that if my sister did come, I would have plenty of food for her, since the sick people couldn't eat anyhow. My sister never came. But I did work in this hospital until we were liberated."

Bertha suddenly straightened herself, smiled, and looked at the students. "The liberation is a special story," she said warmly, as though savoring the feeling again. "The shooting was very close on that day of April 15, 1945. We didn't realize what was happening. I didn't know what it meant to be liberated, because we had no idea what life was really like. I only knew Auschwitz and I only knew being a *Heftling*, 'a prisoner.' Around five o'clock in the afternoon, all of a sudden we heard the microphones. And in German, '*Wir sind schon da; Wir sind schon da!*' We're here! We're here! We've come to free you! We didn't even know what being free meant. Now let me tell you, the most wonderful thing that could happen to a person, were the Americans."

"They came into the camp at five o'clock. By seven o'clock, the camp was filled with nothing but the best. There was all kinds of food. But most of us couldn't eat. The ones who did eat became sick and many of them died. But the Americans were beautiful, beautiful." Again tears filled Bertha's eyes, but they were tears of happiness as she told of the reunion with her sister, the long trek "home" to Czechoslovakia, finding one brother who had survived after being sent to Russia, and her gradual recovery from severe illness. We heard the vow which she made at liberation, that someday she would walk through the gates of Auschwitz as a free person.

The students were smiling with Bertha. Everyone was caught up in her renewed-excitement. During the journey, the students were also touched by Bertha's emotions. After Auschwitz, Dean wrote, "I sat and talked with Mrs. Lautman for more than an hour all about her liberation, her treatment, her long search for happiness. Bertha has let warm light shine upon me, a light radiating from a beautiful and wonderful person."

7

We Must Remember Auschwitz

Sarah Parran knew that her response to this journey would be different from anyone else's. As a sixteen-year-old Episcopalian, her knowledge of the Holocaust had been from books alone. She had not experienced personal loss like Lou, Ronnie, or Bertha, nor had she been aware all her life of the murder of six million Jews.

She had begun to learn about the Holocaust in Mrs. Rabinsky's class at the high school, so whatever knowledge she had was recent and perhaps superficial. Or, so she had thought. As a participant in this journey each day's experience burned into her mind, and she was gripped by an anxiety and tension which never seemed to leave her.

Sarah loved Bertha Lautman. From the moment they met, Sarah had been drawn to the survivor. Wherever Bertha went, Sarah could usually be found, quietly offering her friendship and support. No one could predict Bertha's reactions to Auschwitz or what might happen when she took that final step back into her past. "God, help her," Sarah prayed. "Please help Bertha to be strong."

The evening before our visit to Auschwitz, Bertha spoke to the students. "My heart is heavy," she said. "When I think about tomorrow, my eyes cannot hold all of the tears. But I know this much. God allowed me to live and I now can make my vow come true—to return to that most horrible of places—Auschwitz."

No one slept well that night, and when morning came, the students gathered quickly. "Ray, our guide, has taken good care of us," said Mrs. Rabinsky, "he has prepared box breakfasts which will be distributed at the airport. After breakfast we will be taking a LOT Airlines plane to Cracow and from there we will take a bus to Auschwitz. Please hurry. We have a full day ahead of us."

Sarah's stomach was upset and she knew that she had to swallow hard in order to get hold of herself. The turbo prop plane they were about to board was so small that Sarah feared that the ride would be bumpy. Once on the plane, she eagerly accepted the hard candy which the stewardess offered her.

Everyone was quiet and apprehensive during the flight and bus ride that followed. The minutes were like hours; time was passing very slowly and the bus trip seemed ever so much longer than the scheduled ninety minutes. The open fields of the Polish countryside rolled past the windows and occasionally a small cottage with a thatched roof or a peasant perched atop a horse-drawn cart could be seen.

"How much longer?" someone called out. "Five more kilometers," said Ray. Sarah's heart was pounding and she turned to look at Bertha. Everyone wondered whether this could be the route Bertha had taken to go to work every day, since she was one of the lucky ones whose life was spared simply because she had had enough strength to work for the Nazis. Work, however, was only a temporary reprieve for the prisoners, since they knew that, once their usefulness as workers was gone, they too, would be sent to the gas chambers. Emanuel Ringelblum, a well-known archivist, had used the term "modern-day slaves" about the inhabitants of the ghetto. He had used that term to apply to the restricted hardships of ghetto existence. Sarah wondered how he would have described the conditions after the deportation to the camps. "How would he have portrayed the prisoners whose fates were suspended and whose futures were decided by Nazi bullies armed with whips and guns?"

From the bus, right ahead of us, we could see a fortress of low red-brick buildings. Auschwitz. "So ordinary looking," Sarah thought. "What did I expect?"

The Polish village of Oswiecim, or Auschwitz as it was called in German, is situated about 160 miles southwest of Warsaw. The camp was built on the outskirts of the village, on a marshy tract of land surrounded by an area of swamps, sand dunes, and pools of putrid, stagnant water which caused typhoid fever.

Soon after the defeat of Poland in 1939, as high-ranking Nazis searched for an efficient "final solution" for the Jews, Auschwitz assumed its role of infamy. It was decided that since the Jews were not dying fast enough from starvation and disease in the ghettoes and labor camps, a more efficient method must be devised to conduct large-scale and methodical murder. Thus, May 1, 1940 SS Hauptsturmführer Rudolph Höss received a choice assignment: to turn Auschwitz into a death factory for the Jews.

His first orders were to drain the swamps and enlarge the facilities so that there would be room for everyone: Jews, Gypsies, political prisoners, and opponents to Hitler's regime from other countries. But only the Jews were brought in by the millions for the specific purpose of annihilation. The solution seemed foolproof. Poison gas was ordered through German firms. Delivery was prompt, as the business invoices and records found after the war verify. The gas was piped into what looked like shower rooms labeled, "Washing and Disinfection." Once the people were in, the Nazis themselves controlled the flow of poison gas and the death operation went on unceasingly. After the gassing, the bodies were taken to one of the four huge furnaces, and when they were full the bodies were burned in the open. The transports of Jews from all over Europe to this center of destruction and horror never slackened.

Bertha's parents died in the gas chambers at Majdanek and from their ashes came her determination to confront the past. She wanted their story, her story, to live on in the students.

The main gate of Auschwitz looked like a devil's crown with the words *Arbeit Macht Frei*, "Work Makes You Free," above it. "To the victims who died here," thought Sarah, "this was history's biggest lie." "Are we really prepared for this?" the students asked one another. Everyone was tense and waiting—for what? What would Bertha do? The students held onto her and onto each other as they moved slowly through the gate.

Bertha walked in a daze saying, *Rebono Shel Olom*, "Oh, God of the World."

It was cold, so cold that the students were shivering despite the fact that everyone was bundled up in heavy jackets and hats, mufflers and gloves. It was ironic to think of the prisoners who faced the same bitter weather dressed only in rags. Bertha told the students how she and other prisoners had stood motionless for hours in the worst of weather, waiting to be counted over and over again. "It was senseless and sadistic," she went on, "but we were forced to do the most degrading things by the Nazis. Some of us did not have shoes. I cannot imagine how we could bear to stand in the slush, snow, and biting wind, but we did! It was a miracle."

Standing before the 12-foot-high wire fence, all of the films and pictures we had are seen in books took on a stark reality. We knew only too well that when the camp was full of prisoners this fence had been charged with electricity. Anyone touching it was asking for sudden death. SS men in the watch towers were armed with machine guns to make sure that not one prisoner escaped.

As we made our way through the camp we came upon a guard tower. There was a speaker attached to it and that speaker suddenly took on a face which stared menacingly at us. Kenny was overcome with fear, saying, "I am imagining it, I know, but can't you almost hear the trains arriving with the cattle cars jammed with people? I can almost see the Nazi guards rousting the people into lines, beating anyone who resists, kicking, punching, humiliating their fellow human beings! I'm seeing the printed word *Auschwitz* jump out at me, as it has so many times, from the pages of books. I see hundreds of faces, faces of prisoners full of despair and disbelief. And I see the faces of the machine-like Nazis carrying out their orders, and the faces of their infamous leaders. All of this is flashing in and out of my mind."

Back at the camp, the students followed Bertha through the main street of Auschwitz. They arrived at Block 27, the location for the Jewish Museum, but found it locked. Squatting on the steps, the students waited stubbornly until a guard came to say that the museum could not be opened. We were all outraged and said, "We have come thousands of miles for this day, and you must open the door." Finally the doors were opened, and we were grudgingly allowed to enter. Once inside, we saw what remained of the three-and-a half million Jews who died at Auschwitz at the hands of the Nazi murderers. On display in the museum were children's clothes, a smashed doll, tattered yellow stars which the Jews were forced to wear for identification, *talleisim*, "prayer shawls," a *menorah*, "the eight-branched candelabra"—ancient symbol of light lost in a world of darkness—and eyeglasses, through which people once looked at life when it was still unblemished by Auschwitz. Now, the eyeglasses just lay there, twisted and broken.

The students moved mechanically from one exhibit to another until they stopped transfixed in front of a glass enclosure piled to the ceiling with human hair.

"Good God!" cried Scott. "Look at the cans of Zyklon B, 'Gift Gas.' *Gift* means "poison" in German. How many cans are there? How many died from each can? What a nightmare! Look over there! From the ashes of bones they made fertilizer. I'll never forget this. Never."

The students were so shaken by what they had seen that Mrs. Mann advised that they move on to the General Museum, which had a festive display of flags from countries all over the world. Sarah put into words what was on everyone's mind. "If those countries think they are showing compassion for what happened, it's a big joke." "I agree," said Scott. "Where were those countries of the world when they could have helped? No one cared about the Jews when Hitler first came to power and threatened what he would do. Since few countries opened their doors to the desperate refugees who were trying to leave Germany, Hitler assumed that most people didn't give two thoughts about the Jews, and that he could do whatever he chose to do. By the time the war began, Jews all over Europe were trapped."

"The memory of Auschwitz will always be with me," said Bertha. "This trip back has brought old memories to the surface. Over there is the wall called the *kugelfahng*, meaning 'catching the bullets.' Look at those bullet holes! A prisoner was marched in front of it, sentenced one minute and shot the next. Not by a firing squad. All it took was one German and one gun."

Bertha led the students through the area that had been known as the death block. "This is the Shtai Bunker, a small and dark punishment cell, one square yard. Four to six people were pushed in here, forced to crawl on all fours in order to enter. What did it matter if they couldn't breathe?" Bertha began to sob.

Sarah's insides were churning. "I'm so angry," she said. "I hate the Nazis and their collaborators. How could anyone put Mom Lautman in a hellholl like that? I feel like killing them all!" "Wait a minute, Sarah. Take it easy," Betsy pleaded. "I feel the same way, but that can't erase the past. What *will* do some good will be for us to go home and tell people about this place."

"But I'm so afraid," continued Sarah. "Fear, how do I describe the fear I feel? This could happen again to anyone—me, my family, my friends. Aren't the rest of you frightened? Just see how evil men can become?"

The group later boarded a bus for the short ride back to Birkenau, the extermination camp. Birkenau was separated from Auschwitz by a short road, which for most of the prisoners was the pathway to death. An ominous railroad station at the entrance to the camp was the terminal for human cargo. It was here that the selection process took place. Those capable of work were ordered to go in one direction, the sick, the old, and the children in another. Mothers who clung to their children were either separated by the lash of a whip or sent to be gassed with their offspring. All prisoners were at the mercy of the Nazi on duty, who made the ultimate decision whether they were to live a little longer or die immediately.

"I will never forget the railroad tracks," Mrs. Mann wrote in her journal. "The straight, black lines against the snow, ending at the camp."

"Students, remember this moment," Mrs. Rabinsky said. "Think about how different our entry is into Birkenau from that of the victims thirty-five years ago."

At the Memorial site the students and Bertha read prayers, placed wreaths in memory of the dead, and spoke what was in their hearts. Everyone, including the tour guide, was in tears. Kenny struggled for his control. He was the official photographer and was determined that the eye of his camera would record the overwhelming emotion all felt. Near the site where the crematoriums once stood, Bertha said the Kaddish, the Hebrew prayer for the dead. In choked voices, Lou and Ronnie, the children of survivors, joined in reciting the words of praise for God and for the sanctity of life.

After the ceremony, the group walked from barrack to barrack. Bertha pointed out where she had slept, washed, eaten her meager rations, and worked. Most of the brick structures remained as they were; only the wooden ones had been destroyed. "Over there is the *Leichenhalle*," she said, "the place where the corpses were put before cremation. It was the responsibility of the *Leichen Kommando* to scour the area for corpses and bring them here. I was thirteen and that was my job."

"Forever and ever," Mrs. Rabinsky said to the students, "each of us will remember how we cried together in Auschwitz." Lou spoke words at the Memorial that told us of *Chai*, "life." He said, "All Hebrew words are said to have numerical meaning, and the letters of *chai* add up to eighteen. We are eighteen on this journey. Let us add the dimension of life to the memory of the Holocaust."

We began our trip back to Cracow where we would spend the night. Bertha sat in the back of the bus and the students kept questioning her over and over again. "How did you survive?" Later, the emotions and reflections of the day were recorded in the students' journals.

BOB: As we walked among the barracks and barbed wire, I really wanted to cry, but for some reason, I just couldn't. I guess I couldn't identify with what had happened. But while standing at the Memorial, I thought of my own family arriving at Auschwitz. I thought of my own parents lying dead on the frozen ground. Then I cried.

RONNIE: As we walked away from the Memorial, I could think only of my relatives who died there. Who and what were they? Would I have loved them like I love my living relatives? What effect would they have had on me? Soon, I began to think of my grandfather on my dad's side. I've seen a picture of him. He was a strong man, a good man. Even though I was walking alone, I could mentally see all of my relatives beside me, especially my grandparents. The sorrow I felt slowly left me as I thought of the good things. It seemed as if I remembered my grandfather always smiling. I know I would have loved him. I would have loved them all.

Auschwitz

Cold and wet
Dingy and damp
Rows of buildings empty now
Where is life?
What was done?
Dehumanization, torture, murder.

Innocent people
Beaten and broken.
Homeless, without family, friendless.
Where did they go?
What was their fate?
Persecution, suffering, death.

Lists and records
Tables and charts.
Who shall live, who shall die?
What makes man hate?
What closes his mind?
Ignorance, brainwash, prejudice.

No space, no air
Starvation, disease.
Healthy, weak, old.
What kept them going?
What made them endure?
Hope, faith, prayer.

You and I
Young and bright
We control what is to come
Will we choose prejudice?
Will we choose thought?
Education, openmindedness, thought.

SUE

Why?

Whispered voices loom around
A faint but never-ending sound.
"Don't forget" it seems to say
"I won't," I cry, and start to pray.

"Lord," I pray, "I know you're there
But why, if all your kids are dear,
Did this go on, while You were near,
That Your children died in here?"

The echo whispers, fainter now
"Please don't ask the why and how.
But trust, have faith, and soon some day
You'll be sharing what you've learned today."

And so, my friend, don't ask me why
Six million children had to die.
He knows, and that is all we need.
So listen, closely, then . . . take heed.

AMY

Is He the One

Our Father our King in heaven
He, the one who designed the universe
He, the one who gives us life
He, the one who is my rock and my redeemer
IS He, the one to whom I must give unquestionable faith
He, the one to whom I must turn in the time of great need
He, the one who is omnibenevolent
He, the one who is omnipotent
He, the one who is omniscient
He, the one who shows us what is good and right
He, the creator of Auschwitz?

MARC

8

The Holy Books of Cracow

For the past two years, Jonathan had been on the wrestling team of Heights High. In Cracow, Jonathan wrestled with his conscience. He had been unusually quiet on the bus ride from Auschwitz back to Cracow. We were all drained emotionally. But Jonny kept his eyes on Bertha. He kept nodding as she recalled all of the details of her arrival at Auschwitz in 1942 and the years of her long, bitter imprisonment. When Bertha said how grateful she was that she could say the Kaddish there for her parents, Jonny smiled. He stayed close to Bertha as we walked through the maze of streets in the old Jewish ghetto area of Cracow.

It was strange to see Jonny so serious and intense! He had always been the class clown, the student who would amuse the class with a witty remark, a slick repartee. He was always more jovial than serious, more restless than content. The most serious concern in Jonny's life had been his wrestling. He always got up very early for workouts with the coach, concentrating on nutrition to develop lithe and agile muscles, never missing a scheduled meet on a Friday night. Jonny was a fine student, who did not have to work very hard for good grades. He never seemed to worry a great deal about assignments, or for that matter, about anything in his busy life. Perhaps this is why he seemed so different in Cracow. Was it just the aftermath of Auschwitz with Bertha or was it the sense of futility and hopelessness when he met Mr. Jakubowicz?

Jonny wrote about this encounter: "We will never forget our meeting with Mr. Jakubowicz, the head of the community of surviving elderly Jews in Cracow, the man who told us that no Jewish boy had been born in Cracow for twenty years—the man who pleaded with us to take the sacred books from the small synagogue, because when the minyan passes away, what will happen to the holy books? Who will read them?"

The feeling of finality was overwhelming. Had we not been convinced in Auschwitz of the end of the Jewish people in Poland, we were so in Cracow.

The wall of religious books gripped Jonny. He pulled a worn Gemorrah from the shelf and carefully turned the musty pages as Mr. Jakubowicz asked each of us to carry some of these precious volumes with us to Israel. Jonny was obsessed and he turned first to Lou, then to Bertha, then to all of us. "We've got to take these books out. We've just got to. Can't you see? This is what Hitler wanted, to finish everything, even our prayer books."

True, these books were all that was left. The history of the Cracow community was to be found in these holy books in the synagogue of the great Rabbi Moses Isserles, the fifteenth-century rabbi who codified the Jewish Law. The books were old, very old, and the pages, yellow and a bit torn-up on the edges, were falling out. To leaf through these sacred books is to uncover an entirely different way of life—the life of a once very religious Jewish community in Cracow. These volumes tell the whole story of these Jews and are their only living memorial.

Jonny was ready to carry out this self-assigned task. He would call KLM to see if the airline could ship the books. We could also carry a few books in our hand luggage. Jonny was full of ideas and almost frantic as he took down another Gemorrah, a Siddur, a holiday prayer book.

Mr. Jakubowicz was caught up in Jonny's earnest efforts. He and his wife who had joined him spoke to us in Yiddish. They were so impressed that young people could be so concerned with what had happened to the Jewish community in Cracow. Before we decided what to do with the books, however, Mr. Jakubowicz wanted to take us around the site of the former Jewish ghetto in Cracow. Still holding several prayer books, Jonny followed closely as the elder Mr. Jakubowicz took his cane and guided us through the winding streets. Mr. Jakubowicz explained that with exception of the Remaw Shul, named for Rabbi Isserles, all of the old synagogues are museums. The old synagogues were built into the ground, since an ancient edict said that no synagogue could be built as tall as a Christian church. We visited the ancient Jewish cemetery and saw the worn Hebrew inscriptions on the broken tombstones. All of us recognized what Jonny had felt so keenly: total deterioration and loss.

Soon Mr. Jakubowicz took us to another magnificent synagogue which is now a museum, stately, grand, but empty. In the loft area, probably used for the women's section in times past, were marble tiles and segments of flooring with richly engraved pictures and lettering from previous centuries.

Lou, Marc, Craig, and Amy all began to question our elderly guide. He sadly told us his own story about losing several brothers and sisters in the war, about marrying a widow whose son he helped raise. He said that almost all the young Jews had left Cracow, however. Only the old and the retired constituted the small ailing community that was left—and the sacred books.

We had all listened to Jonny and took a book or two with us but there was no time to crate the entire roomful of old volumes in the Remaw Shul. Jonny never forgot Cracow. He struggled with the notion of finality. He couldn't believe that a thousand-year history of Polish Jewry had come to an end.

Today Jonathan is devoting his life to the study of the holy Talmud in a yeshiva in Hadera, Israel—no more early morning workouts, no dreams of a team win in the wrestling matches. Jonny studies each page with fervor. The lessons in the holy books will never be destroyed.

9

On to Israel

Transportation had been such a major factor during our journey. "I seem to be caught up with the traveling aspect," wrote Mrs. Rabinsky, "rushing, stuffing our suitcases, gathering in lobbies, waiting in front of buses and in airports, joking and joshing. And yet, as we bustle through each departure and arrival, I keep making mental comparisons to the other journeys more than thirty years ago. Is this an obsession to think of Bertha and Sue Beer and Leon Shear and Rose Kaplovitz and the myriads of people being shoved to their departure points, grabbing clothes bundles, squeezing a toddler's hand, standing or squatting in the *Umschlagplatz,* "deportation area," waiting for the rattling empty cars? We had passed the site of the *Umschlagplatz* in Warsaw, which is now no different from any other city corner. The tracks of Birkenau were different. There was a bleak weird emptiness, but the voices were captured and silence screamed. No raunchy jokes, no excited anticipation, just screaming, teeming hordes of humans, spewing from the boxcars. And the SS voices, 'Drop your bundles here! Line up! Raus! Raus!' "

We were now en route to Israel. At the airport in Warsaw everyone giggled and sang, especially Heights High songs and carols as a last goodbye to Poland. The students were talking excitedly with Bertha about the sense of renewal after having visited Auschwitz. "From now on we celebrate *Chai*, life," shouted Scott as we boarded the airplane.

65

The talk was lively as well as sobering on the plane. We were all ready to make the transition from East to West and in the context of our journey, from death to life. Bob later wrote, "After seeing Eastern European Jewry fade into oblivion, it is refreshing and a great relief to be going to Israel where there is life instead of death." Dean's comments were on a more personal note, "We leave for Israel, yet, I'm kind of upset. There is so much more to be seen and taken in. When will be the next time that I'll be fortunate enough to travel to Eastern Europe? From the ruins we are going to the reconstruction. We will see the people who have survived and somehow have put their lives back together. But underneath this all, I feel for my father and his bitterness toward Poland and the Nazis. Words cannot express the sadness I feel. While at the Jewish cemetery in Warsaw, this feeling only intensified. It was heartwarming to know that when those people died, they were at least respectfully laid to rest. But where are the thousands from my father's town? This a question I'm at a loss to answer and I cannot really dwell on it. Nevertheless, it depresses me considerably." Dean wasn't all glum on the plane. Like everyone else he began to talk about our friendships. "If for nothing else, spending hours on the plane gives me the opportunity to talk with people I haven't had a chance to talk to yet. It's such a warm feeling knowing how close so many of us have become in seven short days. These are relationships that are built on such personal experiences that they must last."

Mrs. Mann spoke of her lasting and overwhelming impression after a week in Eastern Europe. "Without doubt, the Jewish nation has been transplanted to another place in time and history." She would write later, "An important culture has vanished from this part of the world, not through natural causes or the evolution of time. One group of human beings has made a judgment on another. The Jewish Museum in Warsaw, the cemeteries in Cracow and Warsaw, the synagogue in Prague, all record the death of a people and a culture, all of the horrible moments of the German onslaught and terror. But what will happen in a few years? In areas where there are no Jews, will they become an archaic curiosity? Fifty years from now, how many people will want to know or care? Or, have the victims become martyrs and will they arouse more compassion and interest because they no longer exist? Cynthia Ozick said something about this in her recent article, 'All the World Wants the Jews Dead,' where she writes about the special place that Jews have always held in the prejudice and ignorance of some people. She wonders if it would have been different if the Jews had vanished from the face of the earth within the last 3500 years. 'Maybe then,' she muses, 'would the Jews be revered for their contributions to society akin to what we say about the glory that was Rome or the advanced civilizations of Ancient Greece? Instead, we are pitied but only up to a point. Has the world changed at all?' "

> Shofar blowers
> Young messengers
> Return and shout
> The World must know
> Truth.

Shout we did when we landed for a two-hour stop in Zürich. "I felt a relief that I could identify only as freedom," wrote Marc. "I no longer had to worry about talking to the 'wrong' people or about being watched by a government agent." Glorious, sumptuous, noisy Zürich airport! Our first taste of familiar Western extravagance in more than a week. What a joy and sense of relief to have the comforts we're so used to from home. Sarah and Janet took advantage of the excellent phone service and immediately called their parents. The round-robin phone calls to the other parents would begin. Washrooms, spotlessly clean, were a special comfort. Until departure we all roamed through the elegant shops and boutiques in the airport. Prices were exorbitant, but we treated ourselves to delicious Swiss chocolate candy bars. Swiss Air stewards served an elegant buffet. We couldn't believe the abundance of food for a "petite" lunch: juice, coffee, assorted sandwiches, pastries, and fruit.

Suddenly, as we waited to have our suitcases checked at Swiss Air, we heard orders blared out in German to deposit our hand baggage and to proceed to a large room to have our luggage checked. There was confusion and anxiety because many of us did not understand the directions. This was our first chance to see our bags which had been shipped through from Poland. Security was really tight.

Every item of our belongings was examined. Yet, it was a comfortable feeling to know that the precautions were for the benefit of us all. Mrs. Mann remarked, "Look, we're in the airport en route to Tel Aviv. What was it like in those cities and depots of Eastern Europe when orders were shouted and there was confusion and anxiety, but people knew that to disobey meant death? We are fortunate to live in freedom."

Tension mounted on the second leg of our journey to Israel. We were due to arrive in Tel Aviv at 7 P.M. Israeli time. We were all anticipating something very special, but we didn't yet know what it would be. There would be family reunions. Mrs. Rabinsky's daughter, Rena, her husband, Marc, and baby granddaughter, Leora, would surely be there from their kibbutz home in the Negev (southern area of Israel). Mrs. Lautman would see her brother, Shimon, his wife, and their married son and daughter for the first time in six years. Jon and Craig would be welcomed by their sisters, Sharon and Shoshana, who were both studying in Israel. Marc expected a host of friends from every major city at the airport. He had met them through camping conclaves sponsored by an international Boy Scout organization.

Arrival in Israel

All of our expectations did not prepare us for what awaited us on our arrival at Ben Gurion Airport in Lod, Israel. A special guide and a reporter from a large daily newspaper, *Yediot Achronot,* "The Latest News," were waiting at the bottom of the stairs as we deplaned. It was dark already and we were guided by airport lights. The reporter hurried our group under the wings of the plane, snapped flashbulbs, and tried to record our excited cries and comments. What VIP treatment we were accorded in the special guest lounge at the airport! Mrs. Miriam Meyohas, Program and Seminar Director for the World Zionist Organization had arranged a beautiful reception. We all crowded around Bertha's family. Everyone hugged Sharon and Shoshana. Rena and Marc's baby belonged to us all! Marc's friends and their families were our friends, too! We laughed and cried as we embraced relatives and friends. A reporter interviewed the students. He, too, was a survivor of the Holocaust. He probed for responses and reactions to what we had seen in Eastern Europe. Two days later, a long article accompanied by a picture would appear prominently in the Israeli newspaper. We were introduced to Marlene Singer, our own personal program coordinator and guide for the next six days.

Later on, the students recorded the intensity of their emotions on our arrival in Israel. Jon wrote, "Never before in my life have I experienced excitement as that which I felt when we arrived in Israel. This feeling of elation is hard to put into words." Jay, too, had shared this excitement, "On our plane to Israel, I felt great. It was the first time in six days that I felt comfortable with so many people. It felt good to pray on the plane and to have other people praying, too. Everyone in our group was excited when we landed at Ben Gurion Airport." "Landing in Israel this time held many more charged feelings than the last time I was here," wrote Dean. "Such ecstatic feelings of happiness and joy. Tears flowed. Our journey's importance is already recognized here. Educational and government organizations have arranged our entire stay in Israel, six fully-packed days of tours and seminars. To be the center of such excitement is really overwhelming." "We are in Israel, finally," wrote Lou. "I felt that today's travel was a retracing of the steps to freedom after liberation. Leaving Warsaw, it was such a wonderful feeling not to be afraid to wear my *keepah*, "head covering," or to pray in public. I was liberated from feelings of hostility. I set foot in my free homeland, where everyone has something in common with me and we are all one. We traveled from the destruction of the Jews in Europe to the construction of the Jews in Israel." Sue wrote that she was overcome with feelings. "I felt as though I were swelling with pride, strength, and power. In Israel, I was returning home after a long vacation. If only my parents lived here."

10

Christmas in Bethlehem

Five cities in one day! Who would believe that we had left Warsaw at six in the morning, refueled in Geneva, stopped for candy bars and a plane change in Zurich, landed in Tel Aviv, settled in Jerusalem, and kept our promise to be part of the Christmas Eve celebration in Bethlehem!

No one spoke of exhaustion. Our spirits were recharged by the fervor and excitement of the crowds. Thousands and thousands of people were there, an ingathering of nationalities from all over the world. Some of us recognized phrases in French and Spanish among the babble of voices. Our purses and tote bags were checked by Israeli soldiers before we could surge ahead with the multitudes going to the center of Manger Square. Kenny commented later on the precautions taken for safety reasons, "The security was extremely tight. We had to show our invitations to the ceremony and our passports to soldiers who carried *uzzi*, "submachine guns." We saw many armed guards, including two on a nearby rooftop. The soldiers are no older than I am, but I realize that it must be that way, that they must be constantly on the alert. It is scary."

Moods changed quickly, however, to amazement and joy as we crowded together in front of a giant television screen in the center of Manger Square. Strings of sparkling colored lights spiderwebbed from rooftop to rooftop. Towering above the square on one side of the screen was a huge Christmas tree, blazing with light and bright

71

garlands of paper. "It was bewildering and beautiful all at once," wrote Sue. Portions of the service of the Midnight Mass which was being celebrated inside the Church of the Nativity were projected on to the massive television screen to accommodate the crowds who couldn't possibly enter the church. Suddenly Sarah fell to her knees, her eyes transfixed to the screen, and began to murmur the Latin phrases of the Mass which were intoned by the celebrant. We all recognized that this must be a very special moment of religious feeling for Sarah and Betsy.

All of us stood closely together, offering warmth and friendship to Sarah and Betsy. It must have been very difficult for them to be separated from their families on Christmas Eve. Scott noted the uniqueness of this moment, especially for Sarah. "I was so happy for Sarah. Here she was in Bethlehem on Christmas Eve, at Mass. This night she will remember forever. Sarah prayed and cried. Everything was so magnificent." Hours after our return to Jerusalem, Sarah tried to recapture and hold on to those moments of magnificence and joy. "Tonight was Christmas Eve and I think that it has been one of the most beautiful nights of my life. A year ago, if anyone had told me that someday I would be in Bethlehem for Christmas Eve, I would have told them that they were crazy. As I stood and watched the Midnight Mass in Bethlehem, I felt totally different. All of my tiredness vanished. I realize what a lucky person I am to have had an opportunity to be there and to be as blissfully happy as I am. Everything was just so beautiful and perfect, especially the Mass being said in Latin. I could have stayed forever. I was just overcome with happiness and love for the world. For a little while I escaped the sad reality of our trip."

Sue expressed many of our emotions when she wrote, "Christmas Eve in Bethlehem enabled me to look at Israel from a different perspective. Not only is Israel central to the Jewish people, but it is the motherland of three of the world's major religions: Judaism, Christianity, and Islam. The multitude of Christian pilgrims we encountered in Bethlehem were in my Jewish homeland to celebrate one of their holiest days, the birthday of their Lord. It's amazing to think that while this Christian holy day was in progress, Jews and Moslems, a few miles away, were at their holy shrines, the Western Wall and the Dome of the Rock. Bethlehem has opened my eyes to a larger Israel, the universal Israel, homeland of Christians, Moslems, and Jews alike. Tonight, Israel is everyone's home."

Home. "How far away," thought Betsy. Even Craig noticed her loneliness when he wrote, "Betsy was a little upset at not being with her family today." Betsy, the thoughtful, caring, sensitive student. She had first endeared herself to her teacher early in the semester when she had spoken about the importance of her family in her life. She had cried in class when Bertha Lautman spoke of her father's last blessing to her before they were separated. "I've never really been away from my parents or brothers and sisters for any long period of time. I can't even imagine what it would be like," Betsy had remarked to Bertha as we came together after class. To the Rev. and Mrs. Fred Jenkins, Betsy's parents, family closeness and sharing of experiences were top priorities in raising their children. In addition to their own children, the Jenkins family had welcomed foster children, many of whom came from broken homes and crushing emotional experiences. These youngsters had found love, comfort, and guidance in the Jenkins home. So, being away from her family at Christmas time was especially difficult for Betsy. "Perhaps," we thought, "that is why her reaction to Bethlehem contained notes of sadness and disappointment." She wrote, "On looking back to Christmas Eve, I was somewhat disappointed about Bethlehem, because it was not what I had expected."

"As I walked up the hill leading to Manger Square outside the Church of the Nativity, I wanted to feel excitement at being in Bethlehem on Christmas Eve. I was fascinated watching Mass being said in the church even though I couldn't understand a word of it. But it was a Christmas Mass and that in itself was special. I am sorry that we did not see the interior of the Church of the Nativity because I am certain it is beautiful. I did not, however, feel the Christmas spirit I have felt in years past at home with my family."

Each of us tried to bring a bit of home to Sarah and Betsy as we gathered mementoes to stuff into two Christmas stockings for them early in the morning on December 25th. Cologne, candy, wash and dry towelettes, hair clips, and assorted things were stuffed into two white stretch socks. A little bit of hilarity, a few tears, friendly hugs and then we left, still fatigued, but ready to begin a day of lectures and discussions.

11

Jerusalem, Yad Vashem

Christmas morning in Israel! Sarah and Betsy shrieked with delight when they saw the two stockings. Being away from their families over the holiday might not be so lonely after all.

"You're all wonderful. Thanks for remembering us. Where did you find such neat presents?" Both girls could not believe that plans for this celebration had been made without their knowledge and that their presents had been purchased one at a time all the way from Prague to Bethlehem.

"Let's eat breakfast", Sarah said. "All of this activity has given me a terrific appetite."

The table in the dining room of the youth hostel was loaded with typical Israeli breakfast foods—juice, rolls, hard-boiled eggs, cucumber, tomatoes, and *leben* (was it yoghurt or sour cream?). Everything looked so delicious that the students heaped their plates to overflowing. Between giggles and bites the food disappeared. "Let's hurry, folks. The bus is waiting for us," Mrs. Rabinsky said.

"What would we do without the three moms keeping us on time?" Sarah said. She was in an exuberant mood. Wasn't it marvelous to be in Jerusalem on Christmas morning?

Thus began the first full day of activity in *Eretz Yisrael*, the "Land of Israel." The students knew that the schedule for the next day and a half included lectures and a tour at Yad Vashem, the Memorial to the Six Million Jewish victims. There were many questions.

"Is it true that dignitaries and heads of state from every country

75

come to Yad Vashem when they visit Israel? What will we do there? Will we have any free time?"

The teachers listened to the questions and then replied. "Although we visited Yad Vashem before, this time is different since we are coming as guests of the Jewish Agency, our sponsoring group here in Israel. We will probably get VIP treatment, and yes, all leaders *are* taken to Yad Vashem. Don't you remember seeing the pictures of Anwar Sadat walking through the museum during his historic visit to Jerusalem?"

"We will now go directly to the educational wing of Yad Vashem where we will meet Dr. Yitzhak Arad, chairman of the Directorate." The concept for the Memorial began with one person presenting the idea to the Jewish National Fund during the war. Everyone agreed that there should be a central repository for documents and testimony, but no one knew where that should be, since there was no state of Israel at that time.

Amy remarked that Dr. Arad must be an important man in Israel. "Not everyone who comes to Yad Vashem gets to meet Dr. Arad. He is a scholar and an authority on the Holocaust. We are hoping that he will allow us to visit the private archives that are open only to researchers and staff."

"Well, I hope we'll have some time for ourselves," Janet said. "I would like to think about something else beside the Holocaust. We have been getting very little relief from a heavy subject."

"I know how you feel, dear," said Mrs. Mann. "Our intake of information has been concentrated. However, Israel presents another side to the Holocaust story. Up until now, we have been submerged in the despair of Eastern Europe where the Jewish communities have been all but erased. But now, we are in Israel, the land of rebirth, and we will be looking at the same subject from a different perspective."

The bus moved slowly up a winding hill. At the top was the Department of Commemoration of Yad Vashem. The crisp air of Jerusalem was so inviting that the students took deep gulps of it before moving into the building.

Dr. Arad was waiting. A distinguished-looking man with grey hair, he greeted the students and began to tell the story they had come to hear.

"Yad Vashem came into being in 1953 when the Martyrs' and Heroes' Remembrance Law was passed unanimously by the Knesset. Certain objectives for this Memorial were set forth. The task of Yad Vashem is to gather into the homeland material regarding all the members of the Jewish people who laid down their lives, who fought and rebelled against the Nazi enemy and its collaborators. We also strive to perpetuate the memory of all of the communities, organizations, and institutions that were destroyed because they were Jewish. We honor the struggle of the people and the heroism of the fighters who rose up and kindled the flames of revolt to save the honor of their people.

"When you leave this building you will walk along a beautiful tree-lined path that leads you to the Museum and the Memorial Shrine. We call this the Avenue of the Righteous Among the Nations. Each tree has been planted by an individual who risked his own life to save Jews. To date, more than 2,250 individuals and members of their families have been granted this recognition. Several hundred cases are still under examination."

"How are these people found?" Marc asked.

"The initiative to have an individual honored by Yad Vashem is usually taken by the people who were rescued. During the past year, many such requests have come to Yad Vashem from all over the world. Both individuals and groups are recognized. A questionnaire is submitted that concentrates on the following information: contact between the rescuer and the Jew, description and the aid rendered, the motivation for the rescuer. Was it friendship, humanitarian motives, religious conviction, financial remuneration, or what? Questions are asked regarding the dangers faced by the rescuer and the attitude of the rescuer's family. In the cases of survivors who live abroad, testimony is verified at Israeli embassies and consulates all over the world and then forwarded to Jerusalem."

Betsy raised her hand. "Dr. Arad, how can you equate rescue efforts? Haven't some people done more than others?"

"Of course. We have to evaluate all of the information that we receive. There are three honors depending on the extent to which the rescuer risked his life. The highest honor is to receive a specially engraved medal and the right to plant a tree at Yad Vashem. The medal has a Hebrew inscription that reads on one side 'As a token of the gratitude of the Jewish people.' On the opposite side is a rabbinic saying that reads 'He who saves one life, it is as if he saved an entire world.' Those in the second category receive a certificate and the right to plant a tree while those in the third category receive a certificate.

"Now, may I ask you to follow me to the Yad Vashem Library, and then we will visit the archives in our vaults below. I will ask you to meet again in these rooms for a debriefing on what you have seen. Then I will address you on the subject of the image of the Jew in Nazi ideology. Mr. Shalmi Barmor of our staff will speak to you about patterns of Jewish response. He will explore some of the myths that have sprung up regarding the Holocaust. His intent will be to explore generalizations that people make and explain to you how the Holocaust must be viewed as a human occurrence. We cannot say that all Jews were naive. We cannot say that all Germans were evil. The Holocaust happened to people and it brought out the very best and the very worst of human qualities. But now, let us go to the library."

Craig was overwhelmed by the library stacks crammed full of Holocaust literature. "How many books are there in this library?" he asked.

"I can answer that question," said Ora Alcalay, the librarian. "The Yad Vashem Library has approximately 50,000 volumes in fifty languages and thousands of periodicals. Our library receives two hundred and fifty publications regularly, and it also has extensive collections on anti-Semitism."

"Mrs. Lautman, Mrs. Mann, Mrs. Rabinsky, look what I found!" said Lou, beside himself with excitement. "Here are pictures of my grandparents—right in this book!" Everyone ran to look and share in the thrill of Lou's discovery.

The students were taken down to the lowest level of the building into the closed temperature-controlled archives. Rows of vaults that contained precious eye witness accounts and personal statements filled the room. The testimony was in the form of diaries and memoirs—valuable documents that could clarify many events that had taken place. Freedom Fighter Hannah Senesh's diary was there along with the records of Warsaw Ghetto archivists Chaim Kaplan and Emanuel Ringelblum. Sue thought about the value of these documents and she trembled with excitement. It was like being at center stage in a very important play, except that this wasn't make-believe. Here she was in Jerusalem in the exclusive archives of Yad Vashem. She was looking at original material that would be cherished by Jewish historians for all time to come. What would her friends say if they could see her now!

At lunch, the students talked about the morning programs. They realized that they were becoming very critical of speakers and presentations. Jay Shifrin commented on Mr. Barmor's presentation to the group. "I thought that was a very meaningful discussion on the *Judenrat*, "the Jewish Council," that was forced to act as a liason between the Nazis and the Jewish Community. They had to do the Nazis' dirty work."

"They could have refused," said Scott.

"Then you weren't listening," replied Amy. "If you were a leader and refused to serve, the Nazis might kill you and your family. And even if they didn't, you would have a guilty conscience—your refusal might mean that someone else would take the job. Would that someone else care about the people and do the same kind of job you could do?"

Adam Czerniakow, the leader of the Judenrat in the Warsaw Ghetto broke under pressure. When he received orders to step up the deportation quota to 10,000 people a day, he committed suicide. Was he a hero or a traitor? Could he have helped his fellow Jews by staying alive?"

"I wonder what I would have done," said Kenny. "The responsibilities of leadership are awesome. Would I have accepted a position of leadership if I knew about the camps and the ovens? What if I didn't know and thought it was simply a question of waiting out the Nazis? Would I help to organize the Jewish community in the ghetto? But then what would I do if I found out the truth about the deportations? Would I tell the people to refuse to go and risk being killed myself? There were so many moral judgments to think about."

Betsy agreed that the subject had been interesting, but she admitted that she kept falling asleep.

"Let's call ourselves the 'Journey of the Unconscious,' " said Marc, who was exhausted.

"I'd like to share the way I am feeling," said Betsy. "I am tired of hearing the same story over and over. Maybe there is a point past which the sights you see and the information you receive about the Holocaust, or anything you are saturated with for that matter stops making an impression. If that is so, I am beyond that point."

Sue answered, "If what you are saying is true, Betsy, could this be the way the German people felt about the brutality of the Nazis? Or the soldiers about their leaders and what they were told to do? It is the old story. No one is responsible. Everyone says he was forced to do what he did. Well, I think they became immune to evil. They passed that certain point. What began as inhuman behavior became the normal way to act."

"Maybe you are right," said Betsy, "but I am being honest. I have reached the point where I am not shocked by anything I hear or see."

Later that afternoon Betsy thought about what she had said. As she walked through the museum she saw the permanent exhibition of authentic photographs, artifacts, and documents that told the story of the destruction of European Jewry. There were many displays that she had seen before, and she fully expected to go through the exhibit as quickly as possible. But she could not. She found herself lingering over many of the familiar pictures and many more that she had not seen before. There was something so powerful in the way this material was presented. She forgot that this subject had bored her this morning.

As they left the museum everyone was silent. "Those pictures were too much," Bob whispered to Ronnie. "I felt like I was choking in there." Ronnie understood. He had cried unashamedly at the scenes of old people in the ghetto. They could have been the grandparents he never knew. All of the stories that his mother had told him were buzzing around in his head.

It was almost time for the memorial ceremony and the group made their way to the shrine. As they walked through the massive gates, the students stopped and stared. The inside of the hall was like a tomb; with walls of huge stone boulders that seemed to reach down and enclose them. Inscribed on the gray mosaic floor were the names of the twenty-two largest concentration and death camps— Treblinka, Auschwitz, Bergen-Belsen—each one a hell on earth. Near one corner of the hall was an eternal light in the shape of a broken bronze cup. Nearby was a vault in which ashes from many mass graves had been placed.

The symbolism and the atmosphere heightened the tension that everyone felt. The ceremony was about to begin. Marc, Dean, and Sue stepped out on the floor while the rest of the group watched from a raised platform. The hall was in semidarkness as the students spoke, softly at first and then vibrant and strong. "I looked for the Jewish communities in Eastern Europe," Marc said, "but they were gone. I came to Israel to find the remnant of the Jewish people; and I am satisfied that it is here. Israel signifies life!"

Sue's voice, clear and sweet, lifted in song. The words were those of the Jewish Partisan's song—the melodic message of spirit that swept through the ghettos of Poland.

> Never say that there is only death
>   for you.
> Though leaden skies may be concealing
>   days of blue—
> Because the hour we have hungered
>   for is near;
> Beneath our tread the earth shall
>   tremble. We are here!

In recalling this moment, Dean wrote in his journal: "Her voice echoed all around me and the words bounced off the walls and became a part of me. Here in Israel people are working toward the establishment of a stable Jewish nation. You could see it and feel it all over. I was so proud to be there."

The day's activities were remembered by Kenny: "Today we heard Ephraim Zuroff of Yad Vashem speak about America's response to the Holocaust. It was so worthwhile for me! He talked about the discriminatory immigration laws of the 30s and 40s and how our government could have rescued refugees but didn't. He told about how disorganized and powerless American Jews were in their attempts to help their fellow Jews—not like today when Jews all over the world are united in their determination that Israel survive as a strong and free nation."

Believe it or not—we left Yad Vashem in the early afternoon and had several free hours in Jerusalem. A whole free day was coming up the next day and we were all making plans how to spend it.

12

Jerusalem, a Free Day

"Where shall we go first?" Kenny asked at breakfast. "We have a whole day ahead of us and no schedule to tie us down. We can do whatever we want to for a change."

"It hasn't been so bad," said Janet. "I am even getting used to gulping breakfast and running for that 8:00 A.M. bus. Besides, think of all the places we have been in the last week and a half."

"That's the trouble," Amy chimed in. "I *am* thinking. I have got lots of bits and pieces in my mind—like a kaleidoscope. Today I want to go slowly and stop when I see something I am interested in."

"O.K. let's decide. What is going on in Jerusalem today? The Sabbath day is a day of rest, so the Jewish stores, museums, and public buildings are all closed. Most people don't work. Instead, they are relaxing with their families or visiting friends; religious Jews go to synagogue."

"I want to go shopping in the Arab market."

"I want to visit Mea Shearim, the ultra-orthodox section of the city."

"I want to walk around the Knesset."

Ideas came from all directions. "Listen folks," said Mrs. Mann, "I suggest that you team up and go in groups. That way you can pursue your own interests. Mrs. Rabinsky will remain here at the Kiryat Moriah, Mrs. Lautman is at her brother's house in Natanya, and I'm going visiting. My friend's daughter has moved to Israel and I would like to find out how she learned the language, set up an apartment, and found a job all in a few months. Talk about determination! I'm not sure how to reach her place, but I will ask some friendly Israelis. There is always someone around who speaks English. See you all later."

Kenny began to organize. "Who is going with whom? Let's start out on our own and we'll regroup tonight at supper. In the words of our famous taskmasters, 'Remember everything you do, kiddies, so you can write about it in your journals when you come home tonight.' "

Once they moved outside, the students were eager to be on their way. The sun was shining and the air was crisp and clear high up in the Judean hills. The Journey of Conscience group was about to discover Jerusalem!

Jerusalem . . . city of majesty and mystery . . . since the time of King David, the attachment of the Jewish people to Jerusalem has remained unbroken . . . through centuries of dispersion to the far corners of the earth, they prayed for a return . . . capital city of the State of Israel since 1948 . . . seat of the President of the State, the Knesset, government, Supreme Court, Chief Rabbinate, Hebrew University, Israel Museum . . . The site of holy shrines for three major religions . . . for Jews, the Western (Wailing) Wall, remaining relic from the days of the Second Temple two thousand years ago . . . for Christians, the Church of the Holy Sepulchre which holds the tomb of Jesus . . . for Moslems, the Mosque of El-Aksa and the Dome of the Rock from where Mohammed is believed to have made his flight into heaven . . . For nineteen years, between 1948-1967, Jerusalem was divided in two, Israel and Jordan . . . barbed wire and concrete walls separated the two parts . . . Jordanians did not allow movement from one part of the city to another . . . After the Six-Day War in 1967, Jerusalem was reunited . . . today this vibrant, exciting city thrives on coexistence between Jews and Arabs, members of the three religious faiths, and the religious and secular way of life.

Ronnie led the group of ten students who decided to stay together for the day. "I am glad we have some decent weather for a change.

No one told me that the rainy season in Israel is from November to March," he said.

Scott agreed. He had thought that yesterday's bus ride to the John F. Kennedy Memorial was a waste of time. "I couldn't see out of the windows. It was raining in torrents, and I got soaked. You're expecting me to rave about the day after being so uncomfortable?"

"Are you spoiled," Sue teased! "Didn't you like the stop we made at the Holyland Hotel? That scale model of the way Jerusalem looked at the time of King Solomon was unbelievable!"

"Yeah, Scott," added Jay. "You sure dug into those cookies that the teachers brought for us in Mea Shearim!"

"I will bet you could have done without our first visit to the Wall, too."

"All right" Scott answered. "Lay off, all of you. I guess I was irritable from being so tired. I am not used to getting by on so little sleep." He thought a moment. "The visit to the Wailing Wall *was* good even if we had to walk in the rain to get there. There was so much excitement with all of those Yeshiva boys taking time out from their studies to welcome Shabbat by dancing and singing. The electricity of their energy touched everyone and I got caught up too. The rain didn't *completely* dampen my spirits."

"Here we are—at the Old City." The same high walls, built by the Turkish Emperor Suleiman the Magnificent in the sixteenth century, enclosed the Old City today. In those old days, almost no one dared to live outside the walls because it was too dangerous. Then, in 1860, Sir Moses Montefiore, an Anglo-Jewish philanthropist, encouraged people to venture out of the crowded Old Jewish Quarter, to establish settlements beyond the walls, and to begin the expansion of Jerusalem!

The students decided that the top of the wall would offer the best view of Jerusalem, so in seconds all of them had climbed up on the ledge for a march around the city. Kenny's momentary dizziness didn't convince anybody to abandon the caper and off they went (Kenny included!) on an adventure that none of them would soon forget.

The Wailing Wall, the Arab Market, Marc's trip to Tel Aviv, Craig's reunion with his grandmother, Sarah's exhaustion, all of these incidents were all recorded in the students' journals as they remembered this day.

KENNY: The Dome of the Rock is the most magnificent building I have seen. On the inside there is a huge circle of carpets that surrounds the famous rock from which Mohammad rose to Heaven. The stained glass windows around the dome were so beautiful, I could have stayed there all day. Best of all was the Arab market with shops of every kind and merchandise of all shapes and sizes. I became an expert at bargaining. The technique went like this: I was with Ronnie and we worked together. We knew that if one of us criticized the merchandise and prodded the other to leave, the shop owner would come down in price. Our lengthy negotiations paid off because I bought a beautiful Eilat-stone pin for my mother and a *chai*, "symbol of life," necklace for my sister. After a fun-filled but tiring day, we all got dressed up and went to visit the Jerusalem Hilton Hotel.

RONNIE: After seeing Jesus' tomb it struck me that in one day, in less than an hour, I had visited the holy shrines of the three major religions.

MARC: Yesterday afternoon I walked through the streets of Tel Aviv with flowers in my hand. I was on my way to visit my adopted Yemenite family. I knew I was smiling because I felt great! All around me the school children were coming home with their back packs and *yarmulkes*, "skull caps". I could feel Shabbat in the air and I loved it. As I walked across the large concrete play area in front of the City Hall, I could see myself playing Frisbee as I did every night after supper when I lived in Tel Aviv last summer. It all looked so familiar. I climbed the eighty-six steps to my family's apartment and surprised them with my early arrival. From that moment on I was floating. My family and friends in Tel Aviv are some of the warmest people I have ever met and I love to be with them.

SARAH: I knew that I was worn-out but I did not expect to get sick. I slept all day and I really felt grimy. Besides that, I missed all the fun at the Arab market. I really love this country but I feel uncomfortable with the security problems. Young men and women are soldiers—everyone has to serve in the army, and you can't help feeling the danger that could be lurking anywhere. The militant Palestinians will stop at nothing to destroy Israel, but this must never happen, no matter how hard they try. The Israelis have spirit! I am sorry that I missed seeing the city and that I missed the tomb of Jesus. That would have been fascinating. Oh, how I wish I had seen that.

JON: I particiapted in religious services at the Wailing Wall and it was a thrill to see all of the different Torahs. I went from one service to another—the prayers are the same but the customs of prayer differ according to where the people are from. Jews from seventy countries have come to Israel and each group has something to add to Israeli culture. This afternoon I walked through the Old City and went back to the Wall for afternoon prayers. While I am in Israel, I want to see Israelis, not Americans. Nothing will take away the joy I experienced on this Shabbat.

BETSY: As I walked through the dark passages in the old buildings, I marveled at the architecture. It is hard to imagine buildings standing for such a long time. In America, a building that is one hundred years old is unusual, but here in the Old World, buildings and artifacts may be around for five hundred or a thousand years before they are considered old. I am glad I visited the Church of the Holy Sepulchre but I was not happy with the Christian guide and the commercial tone of his explanation. I know that the Christian denominations that maintain the church have a lot of responsibility, but holy places such as Christ's tomb should not be exploited and that's what I thought it was! He was asking for donations! My father is a minister. I can hardly wait to tell him about this!

CRAIG: Constant war wears at the spirit of the people. I visited my grandmother and was able to see what four Middle East wars had done to her.

We have to fight constantly and pay for our freedom. The price is always too high.

13

A Warsaw Ghetto Hero

Kenny Myers often speaks of his first week in the Literature of the Holocaust class. "I couldn't believe the assignment sheet. Three major research papers in one semester, besides readings and reports, group programs and interviews with survivors! I wanted to drop the course immediately, even if this was going to be a 'life experience' and not a traditional high school class." Kenny persevered, however. Maybe it was the "A" he received for his first written effort. He became one of the most sensitive, dedicated students, totally involving himself in the class Holocaust Outreach Program, speaking to school, community, and religious groups of students and adults. Kenny, the athletic team's scorekeeper, choir soloist, news reporter, playground director, popular senior-class member, became an emissary of the Holocaust, emphasizing that, "We, the generation after, must prevent such a tragedy from ever occurring again. We shall never forget." Kenny and Bob, both members of the same class, were co-editors of the *Journal of Testimony*, the first student publication dedicated to recording the experiences of Holocaust survivors living in our city. They were concerned with personal stories of such tragic dimensions that they often found it difficult to edit the numerous accounts written and recorded on tape by the class members. Kenny was particularly impressed by the experiences of the families and young people who fought to survive and retain their human dignity in unbearable ghetto conditions.

It was not surprising, when early on the journey, Kenny asked if he could be one of the students to make a presentation to Antek Itzchak Zuckerman, Warsaw Ghetto fighter and founder of *Kibbutz Lohamei Ha Gettaot* "Ghetto Fighters' Settlement."

We had traveled more than three hours in a mini-bus to reach this beautiful garden-like settlement in the north of Israel. Accompanying us for this special visit with Antek Zuckerman were Gabi Adam, reporter for the youth weekly TV program "Elem V'Almah," and three members of a camera crew. They photographed us boarding the bus, arriving at the kibbutz and speaking with Antek Zuckerman. We didn't know then that this special session was going to be the feature of a *Yom Ha Shoah*, "Holocaust Memorial Day" program on the TV segment two years later.

All of us were awed by Antek, a tall powerfully built man, with thick, grey curly hair, looking much younger than sixty years old. He spoke in Hebrew, with Marlene interpreting, telling us how impressed he was with our mission. His words described briefly the Warsaw Ghetto Uprising in April, 1943. He did not elaborate on his role in this great Jewish resistance. Our students, however, had learned about Antek Zuckerman and Zivia Lubetkin, who became his wife after the war. They had been members of the Deror Youth Group in Warsaw. Together with Mordecai Anilewicz and other youth leaders, Antek founded the *ZOB*, "Jewish Fighting Organization," which organized armed resistance against the Nazis. Because of his physical appearance, he was often able to pass on the Aryan side of the Warsaw Ghetto, gathering small arms and ammunition which he then smuggled into the ghetto through the sewer system. Antek also offered news and clandestine help to many Jews who also passed as Aryans outside of the ghetto. During the valiant uprising which began April 19, 1943, both Antek and Zivia fought against the Nazis. Finally, when Mila 18, the bunker command headquarters of the resistance was destroyed and Commander Mordecai Anilewicz was killed, Zivia Lubetkin and a handful of survivors escaped through the sewers. She remained to fight with partisans in the Polish Revolt against the Nazis in October 1943. Unfortunately, Zivia was ill during our visit and was not able to meet with us.

Both Antek and Zivia were instrumental in founding Kibbutz

Lohamei HaGettaot in 1949. As we marveled at the large expanses of greenery, at the small houses with trellises and plants, blooming even in the cold misty weather, we were told that this kibbutz is a highly-developed, sophisticated farming and small industry collective settlement. After our meeting with Antek, we walked with him to the Ghetto Fighters' House and the Holocaust Museum which is the pride of the kibbutz.

After walking through a corridor with exhibits of pictures of young Zuckerman, Anilewicz, and other ghetto fighters, we gathered in an upstairs corridor to make our floral presentation to Antek. We also gave a donation to the educational center of the kibbutz which publishes documents and books about the Holocaust, especially the resistance movements.

Antek Zuckerman touched our hearts. Jon remarked that Antek was so quiet and humble in his manner that it would be difficult to imagine him fighting in the ghetto. For Sue, Antek was a hero and a celebrity. "Merely being in his presence was an honor in itself," she later wrote.

Three of the students responded to Antek Zuckerman in their dedication speeches. Craig had the most difficult task because he spoke in Hebrew. He told how the nations of the world, even the United States Congress, did nothing of significance to save the millions who perished under the Nazis. He pledged to Antek that the students of the Journey of Conscience would return to the United States to meet the challenge of ignorance about the Holocaust, "to do what we can to influence our legislators, to teach them that the State of Israel must exist, is just, and was necessitated by the Holocaust." Kenny's speech reflected all of our emotions. "We are filled with an indescribable awe and pride as we share this moment," he said. "When we stand here and reflect upon the past, we cannot help but look to the future. We have traveled through Czechoslovakia, Poland, and now Israel, to get a better insight into the Holocaust Era. We stood on the site of the Warsaw Ghetto and wept at the memorial to those great fighters. We have seen the faces of these heroes in books, museums, and now in person. While remembering the dead we must also honor the living. Israel, the heart of three major religions, represents rebirth to the entire world. Five years after thousands of Jewish people were destroyed in Warsaw, Israel, the destiny and homeland of the Jews, was recreated."

During a brief tour of the museum we saw a model of the Warsaw Ghetto and some of the actual weapons that were used during the uprising. We were very sad to learn that of all the resistance fighters who escaped through the sewers, there are less than ten survivors who are still alive.

After the tour of the museum we welcomed the hot coffee and cakes which were served to us in the recreation hall. Our visit to Lohamei Ha Gettaot culminated with a viewing of a most remarkable film, "The 81st Blow." "What an extraordinary film," wrote Janet. "The interminable story in the movie reinforces the unending torture of the Jews in Europe." Our students had seen documentary films in class, but nothing had been as powerful as this movie which was supervised and produced by kibbutz members under the direction of Antek Zuckerman. The film began with scenes of Warsaw and Prague when the Jewish communities were thriving in the first decades of the twentieth century. We recognized places we had visited just a week ago in Prague. While the scenes were rolling, an explanation of the title appeared. A young boy had been beaten in the streets by German guards. He counted eighty blows to his body, but when he tried to tell people about this cruelty, no one believed him. This was the eighty-first blow. Bob's description of the film was most poignant. "I thought I had seen everything until I saw this documentary. There was almost no dialogue, and in this case, the silence complemented the various photos and film clips more than any words could. I guess that the right words do not exist to describe the Holocaust."

"Some of the scenes from the film stick in my mind. I saw a small child, no more than five years old, dressed in a miniature Nazi uniform with a swastika armband and a Nazi banner. It was like robbing the cradle and making a baby into a murderer. What mind could even conceive of this? There was sequence after sequence of Hitler fanning the flames of hatred. No rest between outbursts, no time to let any hatred bounce off. All of it penetrated and made me want to burst. Seeing the entrance of a gas chamber and then having the door shut behind. I got some idea of the sense of horror the victims must have experienced just before they died."

"I had cried at Auschwitz, but I absolutely fell apart during the film. As far back as I remember, no single film or presentation ever moved me quite as much as 'The 81st Blow.' "

The movie left us devastated and the cold, steady rain didn't help to lift our spirits. We were scheduled to leave Lohamei Ha Gettaot and to arrive at the youth hostel, Beit Ruttenberg, in Haifa in less than half an hour. To add to our distress, the mini-bus wouldn't start. We were all tense because several families with high-school children were hosting us for the evening. They would be waiting at Beit Ruttenberg. Marc called Yehoshua Abrahams, a good friend who was now our Haifa contact. "Hurry, call cabs and get here quickly. The families are waiting," instructed Yehoshua. Cabs don't zoom around kibbutzim in northern Israel, but after a restless half hour, we were en route to an exciting meeting with Israeli teenagers. Each family had invited two or three students. Kenny and Sarah went to Danielle's home. "Her mother was lovely, a real Jewish mama. She was very happy to see us and served us a home-cooked meal, consisting of chicken soup and chicken, felafel (pita bread filled with vegetables and spicy fried sesame balls), veal, and fruit. Sarah wrote, "It was fabulous, the first good food that I've eaten since we left America. The best thing was the conversation though. We compared life-styles and countries and national statistics about everything. After dinner, Danielle took us to her friend's house and we met about thirty Israeli kids and had a great time. We just sat around and talked for a couple of hours and listened to records and sang songs. It was one of the most fabulous experiences that I have ever had."

Jay and Janet had been taken by their host to the same party. As we talked later about the enthusiastic gathering, Kenny remarked how our students were surprised that Israeli students know very little about the Holocaust. "They get briefed on it every year, but according to Danielle, it's the same every year. They get a day off for Holocaust Remembrance Day, but the students aren't really involved." "Imagine," said Sarah, "not enough Holocaust studies in Israel. We'll have to work on that."

While the students were entertained by their young friends, Mrs. Mann, Mrs. Lautman, and Mrs. Rabinsky visited Yecheskel and Aviva Taler and their children in Haifa. The Talers had been *shelichim*, "Israeli emissaries," to a youth group in Cleveland and had become very close friends with many of the parents. They were gracious hosts and Aviva is a gourmet cook. What a joy to have had Israeli specialties, hot chicken soup, stuffed peppers, marinated vegetable salad, cooked carrot kugel (pudding), roasted chicken and freshly baked apple fritters with cherry sauce.

We all returned to freezing Beit Ruttenberg, bubbling and exhilarated, anxious to share the stories of our evening in Haifa.

14

Kibbutzim

Despite the freezing cold of the youth hostel, we slept well in wool hats and sweaters, mittens, and scarves. In the morning, pitchers of hot coffee and tea were fragrant and warm. Even the typical youth-hostel breakfast of tomatoes, cucumbers, hard-boiled eggs, and bread was good.

Our bus ride to Tel Aviv and down to the Negev was riotous. We laughed and sang. Avraham, the bus driver, became one of us. He joined in the chorus of a Hebrew song and even in some of the popular American tunes. Suddenly, he asked, "Rock music?" and he produced tapes of the latest hits. Ronnie jumped from his seat, pulled Bertha into the aisle and they began to dance. Betsy later recalled, "The scene on the bus on the way to Tel Aviv was unbelievable! All the teachers and most of us were in the aisles dancing to the music. We were all so relaxed, having the greatest fun."

Kibbutz Alumim

Rain came down in torrents so that it was difficult to appreciate the scenery on our way south. After a brief rest stop in Tel Aviv, we continued on our way to the Negev to visit Kibbutz Alumim, the home of Mrs. Rabinsky's daughter and son-in-law, Rena and Marc, and their baby, Leora. As we approached the kibbutz, about an hour and a half from Tel Aviv, the sun poked through the dismal grey skies. Janet was ecstatic. She couldn't stop admiring the orange groves, fields of cotton, and orchards of small trees which we couldn't identify. She later wrote, "The sun seemed to light up the land. The country is green and growing. A feeling of rebirth was indeed inside of me."

Ronnie was most taken with the kibbutz. Ever since Auschwitz, Ronnie had been quiet, often somber and reflective. It was difficult to confront Ronnie in such serious moods. Ronnie had been the fun-loving mischievous tenth-grader who had come to Heights High the same year as Mrs. Rabinsky. As a member of her sophomore English class, he was hardly a serious student. Two years later, Ronnie had elected the Holocaust studies class "because I want to find out all I can about what my parents and grandparents went through." A very happy fellow, Ronnie proved to be a bright, sincere student. He was one of the first to volunteer for a speaking assignment in the Holocaust Outreach Program. Ronnie enjoyed interacting with people. He was always energetic, enthusiastic, full of life. For Ronnie the first week of our journey was devastating. Visiting the concentration camps, chanting the Kaddish for his grandparents at Auschwitz, examining the Holocaust scenes in museums made Ronnie very depressed. But now on the bus en route to the kibbutz Ronnie came to life. He wanted to see and know everything about this communal settlement. "It's good to see living people instead of pictures and ruins," wrote Ronnie that evening.

Mrs. Mann, Mrs. Lautman and Mrs. Rabinsky hugged Rena at the kibbutz gate. "Hurry," said Rena, "lunch is waiting in Chadar Ochel, the dining hall." We had a delicious and ample lunch, consisting of chicken, beans, cucumber salad, bread, and fresh fruit. For a special dessert we were all invited to Rena and Marc's home.

Rena, known for her exquisite pastries, served chocolate cake, cookies and punch while we learned about kibbutz living from Moti, one of the Chaverim, "kibbutz members". Alumim is situated right near the Gaza Strip. There are about fifty families on the kibbutz, some singles, and more than one hundred young children. Interestingly enough, most of the construction work on Alumim is done by the Arab workmen from Gaza. Alumim is a young kibbutz, only ten years old, with the oldest members in their early thirties. Jay summarized what he learned about the kibbutz. "The kibbutz is a collective village with its own industries and its own store. Everyone shares in what the kibbutz earns. Each family has its private house, but most of the time everyone joins for meals in the large dining room. Children sleep with their parents at night, but during the day they are cared for in children's houses while the parents work. The kibbutz is beautiful and well cared for."

All of the students tossed questions at Moti. "How do Americans used to the luxuries of capitalistic living adjust to this life? Do Americans and Israelis get along together? What does Alumim produce?" Lou was impressed by this settlement of some fifty young families. "Kibbutz life seems strange to one who has lived in an urban setting all his life. Why do people from all walks of life come to live on a kibbutz? There must be many factors indeed. The results seem to be a sense of accomplishment, prestige, and success as a group of special, hardworking, loyal people whose goal is to build up and make fertile the Holy Land of Israel. How I envy these unique individuals!" Craig pulled us back to reality as he talked about the air raid shelters which are situated throughout the kibbutz. "From what I see of Alumim, it is a symbol of the rebirth of the Jewish people. It is alive and bright, and yet, it is near the frontier.

"The brightness and vegatative growth symbolize the joy of life in Israel. The fact that it is so near the frontier reminds us that even while Israel exists, vigilance is the price of freedom." (Ed. note: Now that peace between Israel and Egypt is a reality, dreams of productive co-existence between kibbutz members and their neighbors in Gaza can be achieved.)

"On with the tour of the kibbutz," shouted Ronnie, as Moti led us to the carrot factory. The students were fascinated by this production center which sorts, grades, bags, and packs the kibbutz carrots for export to Europe. Only the second-grade carrots are used for kibbutz consumption. Kenny ran along the factory platform snapping pictures of the students posing with carrots of all sorts. We were given a giant bag to take along with us on the bus. What surprised us was that those in charge of the factory looked younger than most of the students in our group. Bob had the greatest fun. "When we toured the carrot factory I happened upon a behemoth carrot. It was the biggest carrot I had ever seen and suddenly I found that my carrot and I were the center of attention. Unfortunately, my friendship with the carrot was cut short when the poor thing was split in half by Scott. Emergency surgery with masking tape failed and the carrot ceased to exist."

After the carrot factory we toured the immaculate barns with the recently installed electronic milking machines. A twenty-five-year-old *chaver* was running the entire operation. Hundreds of chickens squawked in the *lul,* "chicken houses," just a few hundred feet away. Beyond the machinery sheds were acres and acres of fields. Rena's husband, Marc, was in charge of the avocado fields. He had been up since 4 A.M. and came in by tractor from the fields just in time to say "Shalom" as we boarded the bus to neighboring Kibbutz Yad Mordechai.

Yad Mordechai

We were all refreshed and happy as we left Alumim. Yad Mordechai, another thriving kibbutz, is less than a half-hour drive from Alumim. Named after the Warsaw Ghetto hero and leader of the uprising, Mordechai Anilewicz, this kibbutz was founded by survivors of the Holocaust. A unique museum houses an impressive collection of Holocaust pictures, documents, diaries, and pre-war memorabilia of Jewish life in Europe. The entrance to the museum simulates the underground sewers of Warsaw, through which the defenders escaped the burning ghetto.

Jay was pleased that he was one of the students who were to speak and make a presentation before the statue of Mordechai Anilewicz. Even though Jay was the youngest member of our group, he was one of the most serious students of the Holocaust. He had always questioned the idea of resistance, anxious to know in what camps and ghettoes the Jews had organized against the Nazis. Mordechai Anilewicz became a personal hero for Jay. He listened attentively when Gershon Givoni, a chaver of the kibbutz and a ghetto survivor, spoke about "From the Holocaust to Rebirth." Givoni said when the few survivors joined to organize the settlement shortly after the war, they thought that they weren't worthy to name their kibbutz after as great a hero as Mordechai Anilewicz. Jay wrote later, "I'm sure that they proved they were worthy of the name after the Israeli War of

Independence in 1948. The kibbutz members held off the invading Egyptian army for six days."

After Gershon Givoni's talk, we visited the field which has a simulated battle scene complete with figures of soldiers in the strategic positions they occupied in 1948. The legend in the museum states that each exhibit speaks for those who cannot speak for themselves.

All of us were silent as we climbed the steep winding stairs leading to the outdoor monument which is a greater than life-size statue of Mordechai Anilewicz. Amy placed a wreath of flowers at the base of the statue and Jonathan and Jay each spoke and made our contribution to the education fund of the kibbutz.

Jonny quoted from the prophet Zechariah. "Not by might, nor by power, but by my spirit, saith the Lord of Hosts." "Mordechai Anilewicz was the spirit of the Ghetto Freedom Fighters. They didn't repel the Nazis with their strength or numbers, but with their spirit, their will to survive and to avenge the oppressors of their brethren. Mordechai Anilewicz's dream was for Jewish resistance to become a reality. He did not live to see the impact that his bravery had on those who survived and came to Israel. The strength and spirit of Anilewicz inspired these survivors even during the War of Independence."

Jay spoke of our travels to the monument in Warsaw which honors the uprising led by Anilewicz, to Mila 18, where Anilewicz died, and now to the thriving kibbutz which honors his memory. "I had such strong feelings in front of the statue. We were on a hill and I could see the whole valley. This kibbutz is life and the spirit of Mordechai Anilewicz lives."

Tired, thoughtful, grateful for each unique experience we had shared, we headed back to Jerusalem for our closing dinner in Israel.

15

Amsterdam, Holland

The Anne Frank House

During the Nazi occupation of Amsterdam of 1944, the Gestapo captured a Jewish family in hiding and took them away to a concentration camp. Their furniture and clothing were confiscated, but some books and papers remained strewn about the floor. Among them a tartan plaid-bound diary was found by a Christian friend and kept until the end of the war, when it was returned to the father of its young writer. In time, Otto Frank was to share his daughter's diary with people all over the world.

It is the story of this young girl and her amazing diary that brought us to Holland for the last days of our journey of conscience.

The students, the teachers, and the survivor arrived at Amsterdam's Schiphol Airport, marveling at the display of holiday lights and tinsel. On arrival, we were fatigued and emotionally exhausted, but within a few hours we began to relax and enjoy Dutch hospitality. Our purpose was to learn firsthand about Anne Frank's free and buoyant spirit and of her own story of the Holocaust.

Touring the city, the students discovered that many parts of Amsterdam had been rebuilt since World War II to allow for an interesting contrast between modern and old architecture. The capital city was first mentioned by name in records dated 1434 as "the Dam" built on the River Amster. As early as that, the town had already been a thriving center for at least two hundred years.

In the seventeenth century both population and trade expanded and canals were dug to traverse the city. Merchants were then able to purchase goods anywhere in the world which could be shipped to Holland through the port of Amsterdam and down the canals to their front doors.

Amsterdam's large Jewish population began to emerge at the end of the fifteenth century when Portuguese and Spanish refugees from the Spanish Inquisition were welcomed to hospitable Dutch shores. Throughout the years the Jews had become an integral part of the culture, contributing to the professions, businesses, and the arts, and even lending Hebrew and Yiddish words to the language. Such words as *Mazel Tov* (good luck, congratulation), *l'chaim* (a toast to life) and *chochem* (wise man) are part of the local Amsterdam vocabulary.

It was quite natural that Otto Frank, a banker in Frankfurt-am-Main, Germany, decided to bring his young family to Holland in the autumn of 1933. Hitler's opressive policies against the Jews were alarming to Otto Frank and he was not about to sit and wait to see what would happen. Instead, he brought his wife and two small daughters, Margot and Anne, to the Netherlands, where he opened a small spice importing business. He took in a partner, a Mr. Van Daan. Later, this fellow refugee and his wife and son along with Mr. Dussel, a dentist, were to live with the Franks in their hiding place.

The Frank family's first years in Amsterdam were good, especially for Anne. She loved people. Her friends and her clothes were the center of her life.

In 1940, the Nazis invaded Holland. Otto Frank, foreseeing impending disaster for his family and the Jewish people began to construct a secret hiding place behind his own business office which faced one of the city's tree-lined canals. Taxes on the canal sites were paid according to the width of the house, which meant that the houses had been built pretty much the same way—narrow, deep structures consisting of two buildings connected by a passageway through an inner courtyard. The house at 263 Prinsengracht Street, which was built in 1635, had been remodeled once; the front house had been given a new gable, and the rear house (the annex) had been torn down and replaced by a bigger building. Over the years, this house had been used as a private residence and a place of business. It was to earn recognition and a place in history because of Anne Frank and was subsequently to be called the Anne Frank House.

In 1943, Margot Frank was called for "labor service in Germany." Everyone knew that this meant deportation to a concentration camp. The family moved into the hiding place behind the business office. Anne, thirteen, took with her the diary she had received as a birthday gift from her parents. In it she recorded her innermost thoughts and dreams, chronicling a young girl's transition from childhood to womanhood. She wrote about her life in this secret hiding place which was to her a sanctuary as well as a prison, and she wrote about the people who lived there, of their cramped living quarters, of their restricted existence, of discouragement, but never of despair.

It is not known how the Gestapo found the Franks. Some say that they were betrayed by burglars who had been offered a reward for apprehending Jews in hiding, but no one knows for certain. The family was deported to Auschwitz and then to Bergen-Belsen where the mother and daughters died of typhus. By some quirk of fate, Otto Frank survived and he returned to Amsterdam where he had to face the traumatic past and where he was to read Anne's diary.

The students were all fascinated by the diary. Amy Feinberg had read it so many times that she felt as if the house on Prinsengracht Street were an old friend. She knew beforehand that she would see the mementoes and treasures of a young teenager, who, like herself, was articulate, sensitive, caring, who loved to write and could use words to express her deepest feelings.

"Anne was only a few years younger than we are now when she went into hiding," Amy said to Sarah as they walked up to the house. "I can't imagine spending two of my teen years in a small hiding place, especially living with the fear of being caught."

"I remember reading about how they passed their time," Sarah said. "They couldn't walk around in the daytime because someone might hear them, and they couldn't use the toilet or even take a drink of water. Certainly, they couldn't look out of the window. Someone might see them. They could only sit quietly, do lessons, read, or sleep."

"And at night," Amy said, "all of the windows had to remain tightly closed because of the blackout. If it hadn't been for Elli and Miep, Mr. Frank's faithful employees who brought in food and newspapers, they couldn't have held out for as long as they did. Those two secretaries risked their lives helping the family."

"I'm sure they weren't the only ones who helped the victims," Mrs. Rabinsky said. "There was an active Dutch underground, but they had to fight against unbeatable odds. By the time the Nazis invaded Holland, the German war machine was swift and accurate. As soon as the Nazis entered a town, the Jews were rounded up and deported; 100,000 of them were from Amsterdam."

"Do you think that any survived?" asked Sarah.

"Three thousand returned," answered her teacher. "But it is doubtful if any whole families survived."

The students climbed the precariously steep stairs to the hiding place on the second floor. Huffing and puffing they made their way up and stood before the entrance leading into the annex. But where was it? It was carefully concealed by a bookcase which Anne had described in her diary. No one would suspect that it existed at all if one had not known that it was there. The door was held in place by a hook which could only be unfastened from inside.

Mr. and Mrs. Frank had shared their room with Margot. It was located directly over the offices below and therefore remained out of bounds during the day. The slightest noise might give them away and bring the worst consequence to them all. Remaining on the walls of this room was the small map showing the Allied advance through Normandy. There were also visible pencil marks, recording the heights of growing children. It was in this room that Anne's diary was found.

The next room was Anne's, which she had shared with Mr. Dussel. It was decorated with the pictures that she had cut out of magazines. The lavatory and washing facilities were close by. A steep staircase led to the third floor and the room which served as Mr. and Mrs. Van Daan's bedroom, communal dining room, and living room. The family was able to cook here and burn refuse in the stove since the neighbors were under the impression that a laboratory which had once been in the building was still there.

Next to this area was Peter Van Daan's little room and close by an incline leading to the attic which was used for storage and provisions. The students remembered that Anne had written of her many happy hours there.

As they walked from room to room, the students talked excitedly to each other. Janet couldn't get over the identification she felt with Anne. "I can just see her in her room putting up pictures of Deanna Durbin on the walls. She was a girl just like me, and if circumstances had been different, we could have exchanged places." Jon touched the walls and the sink just to make sure they were real and Lou kept saying over and over, "What must it have been like not to be able to go outdoors—ever? What did she look for when she looked out this window? She couldn't even wave to anyone."

"Well, you know what she did," replied Amy. "To pass the hours she kept a diary, but I'm sure that she wondered for whom and for what reason."

Amy thought about how much she liked working with children. The summers she had spent as a counselor had been some of the happiest times of her life. But she knew that noise and laughter are a natural by-product of children, and she couldn't imagine living the subdued life that Anne had in the hiding place.

Bob said, "I have the same feeling here that I had at Lidice and Terezin. There is a sense of emptiness and unreality about this attic. It's so hard to believe that all there is left of a person like Anne is a diary and a few photographs."

"This is more than remains of many other people," Amy replied. "Anne, at least, retained her individuality and identity. Millions of others died anonymously. In a way, she has assumed their identity for them."

"That's because many of Anne's hopes and ideas for a better world are universal," Bob added. "Young people everywhere can identify with many of Anne's conflicts and feelings. Perhaps we can pick up where Anne left off and carry out some of her dreams."

Mrs. Rabinsky and Mrs. Mann called the students together on the third floor and said, "It's time to make the presentation to the Director of the Anne Frank Foundation." Amy, Jay, and Jon solemnly offered a small wreath and a check on behalf of the group.

Other guests also touring the house moved closer to listen. A hush fell throughout the room as Amy spoke.

"Anne Frank was a child . . . one who loved and learned to hate, a child who lived with joy and learned of death. For two long years Anne Frank lived in this tiny attic with seven other people.

"The diary of this young girl has been printed in dozens of languages, including Braille. For some of us, her diary was our first introduction to the horrors of the Holocaust.

"Anne Frank's story helps us to remember. We remember all the children, in the camps, ghettoes, and the attics . . . all the children who weren't given a chance to grow up.

"But Anne, you are alive! Your spirit lives on in the hearts and minds of the millions who have read your diary. We remember you as one name—you are one child who must represent all of the children who suffered and died with you.

"Anne Frank celebrated life. Anne dreamed of the world at peace, but she never lived to see this peace. Perhaps in our day, Anne Frank's dream will be realized."

After the presentation, people gathered around the students asking questions about the journey and what would happen once the students returned home.

"Actually, what we are doing," Amy explained, "is in the spirit of the Anne Frank House. We want people to act as a result of what they know."

"Let me tell you how the Foundation began," said the Director. "Back in the 1950s, this house was almost taken down by a factory that wanted to build on this site. But the people of Amsterdam refused to let that happen! There was an announcement on the radio about the possible destruction of this building and money began to pour in to save this house. Within hours, they collected enough money to buy not only this house, but also the one next to it as well as the adjoining block. It was then that the Anne Frank Foundation was formed."

"What is the purpose of the Foundation?" the students asked.

"We have many goals; we try to draw parallels between what happened during and after the war with situations in the world today. We are committed to fight discrimination with education. We work to further the cause of emancipating deprived people by making them aware of their rights. The Anne Frank Foundation is a constant reminder of the responsibility that each man has to his fellow man."

"So, you want a visit to this house to be more than an emotional experience," said Amy.

"Exactly. Now follow me back downstairs to see for yourselves the many challenges we have to meet."

On the first floor were pictures and diagrams of discrimination in the world and what organizations like the Anne Frank Foundation were doing to fight against it. Holland was facing a crisis of its own since the former Dutch colony of Surinaam had become independent, and one quarter of the natives had emigrated to Holland. For the first time, the Dutch people were facing problems of racism and the Anne Frank Foundation was deeply involved in many educational projects to meet the situation head on.

Bob, remembering a display in this room, wrote about it later on in his journal: "One thing in particular stood out for me at the Anne Frank House. In an area on the first floor there was a wall hanging presented by a group of children from Hiroshima, Japan. A young girl who had survived the atom bomb, but had developed leukemia as a consequence, had kept a diary of her feelings and hopes during her illness. Her story attracted worldwide attention and the people of Japan gave her moral support and encouragement. A legend grew up about her which said that if the girl folded ten thousand paper doves she would overcome her illness and live. For a while it appeared that she would succeed in this endeavor, but when she was just short of a thousand, she died. Thus, there were two Anne Franks, worlds apart, yet very much the same. I felt honored to visit the Anne Frank House."

The Sephardic Synagogue

"Where do we go now?" the students asked Robert, our Dutch guide, as they left the house on Prinsengracht Street. "Any place we visit will be an anticlimax after the Anne Frank House," they felt.

"Wait and see," said the guide. "You will be surprised."

Later that day, the bus stopped for another visit. "What! Another synagogue!" the students chorused. "We must have stopped to see every single one in Europe!"

The guide smiled and said, "I hope that you are not too tired to come into this one. This is a lovely Sephardic synagogue which was built when this congregation absorbed three smaller synagogues."

"What are those coats of arms?" Sarah asked the secretary of the synagogue who was the guide inside the building.

"The large pelican nourishing the three smaller ones is symbolic of our merger with the three smaller synagogues. The second coat of arms is a phoenix rising from out of the ashes. Is this not what our brave Jews did when they survived the Spanish Inquisition and went underground in order to survive?"

"Were they Marranos? asked Betsy.

"Yes, they were secret Jews. Their double life was exceedingly dangerous because if they were found out, they would have been tortured and probably killed. Sometimes three generations would pass before a family could escape. They came to Holland because here we had religious freedom. Look around you. Have you seen another synagogue like this one?"

The students stood speechless before the grandeur of the huge sanctuary with its enormous chandeliers holding nine hundred candles.

"There are no electric lights in here, or heat for that matter. In the olden days, we held services in here, regardless of the weather. Now we meet somewhere else in the winter and return here in the spring for Passover."

Janet asked, "How many people come here for services?"

"This is something sad to relate. Before the war, we had 6,000 members. But not many of us are left—perhaps 600 at most. Here is our Holy Ark that holds the Torahs. The Ark is fashioned of precious wood brought from Brazil three hundred years ago. Our synagogue is blessed with seventy Torahs and we have a special room for them that I will show you."

"How did the Torahs stay safe from the Nazis?" Jay asked.

"The Dutch people kept them safe for us. Now we share the Holy Torahs with Jews in other countries. We have sent twenty Torahs to the United States and Israel, and next week we will send two more to

Moshavim, the farming settlements on the Golan Heights in Israel. It is a miracle that our Torahs have survived. They must be our link with the future. Some of these Torahs are three hundred years old and their robes and crowns are treasures. Many of them are hand-embroidered and the initials of the donors are woven into the fabric."

"The synagogue is gorgeous," sighed Janet. "I wonder what it would be like to be married here by candlelight. In summer, of course!"

The secretary of the synagogue laughed and said, "When one of the Dutch princesses was married, the royal family borrowed some of our chandeliers for the wedding in the church."

"Tell us something about yourself. We've been asking questions about everything else."

"As you know by now, I am the secretary of this synagogue, but I have had my job for only seven weeks. Thirty-three years ago, I escaped from Amsterdam during the war and I have been living in Buenos Aires ever since. I came back because the synagogue needed me."

"How did you feel about leaving Argentina?" the students asked.

"The secretary thought for a moment before he answered. "Well, I had mixed feelings. I lived all of my grown life in Argentina. I am happy to come back but was sad to leave my friends."

"You now have eighteen new friends," Mrs. Mann said.

"Thank you, my friends. Shalom."

16

Heading Home

Everyone slept late in the morning and lingered over the last smorgasbord breakfast in Holland. Still, the seasoned travelers were ready to leave for the airport *on time* to board the KLM 747 for the ninth plane ride of the journey. "It's a nice feeling going home," said Jay. "I'm looking forward to it. I will remember everything I've learned for the rest of my life."

In flight, the plane met with unexpected turbulence, but no one was alarmed. Ignoring the mediocre movie, the students wrote the last pages of their journals. They had been asked to search within themselves for three answers relating to the journey. Their only instructions were to be brief, honest, and sincere.

If this journey has affected your life in any way, tell how.

AMY: I am more conscious of the plight of the Jews in Eastern Europe. I have seen hell with my own eyes at Auschwitz and heaven in Bethlehem and Jerusalem. I knew that spiritually this would be a very moving experience for me.

MARC: The journey has given me a greater insight into the story behind pictures, movies, and books that once had little significance. I never actually comprehended the totality of destruction.

SUE: I have become more strongly Zionistic. I believe in Hillel's saying, "If I am not for myself, who will be for me?"

KENNY: I hope that I will convey more appreciation for what I have. I hope that I can help others to be more grateful for being alive, living in a free country, and having good health. The trip has given me a view of how other people live. Now I know just how lucky I am.

JANET: The trip has given me a greater respect for the value of human life. This journey has taken me through the full cycle of life—birth, death, and rebirth.

JAY: I will try to be less prejudiced from now on, because I have seen what prejudice can do.

DEAN: After seeing how the world stood by and let millions of people be killed, I will never permit myself to remain silent on matters that are occurring today.

SARAH: Bethlehem and knowing Mrs. Lautman . . .

JON: Antek Zuckerman. I felt very proud of being a Jew after talking to him. I feel very strongly about Jewish resistance.

BOB: Climbing the stairs at the Anne Frank House and walking through the hidden passage behind the bookcase. I entered a secret world which was cut off from outside contact.

RONNIE: Arriving in Prague and knowing that our journey was real . . . thinking about my grandparents at Auschwitz.

BETSY: Admiring Amsterdam, the only city that we visited in Europe that supported its Jewish population during World War II.

CRAIG: Walking with Bertha through Auschwitz.

DEAN: Feeling so close to everyone on this trip.

SUE: A determination to fulfill my pledge to pass on what I know.

KENNY: I want to start spreading our message around to everyone I can and tell them what a fabulous experience this was. And I want to tell my parents how much I love them.

JAY: The sorrow, the hatred, and the joy. I will always remember the places where I cried and the places where I laughed.